D0611287

This is the
Maine Coon Cat

Front cover: Arden's Manitou of Schick, a red mackerel tabby male pictured at eight months of age. Breeder: Carol Knowles. Owners: Sharyn and Richard Bass. Photo: Jan Carson, "Images by Jan," Sterling, Virginia.

Title page: Maine Coon Cats are a natural breed; i.e., man did not interfere with their development. Nature equipped these cats with all of the necessary physical characteristics that they would need to survive the cold, rugged New England climate. Photo: Ron Reagan.

The portrayal of feline pet products in this book is for general instructive value only; their appearance does not necessarily constitute an endorsement by either the author or publisher.

The following photographs by Ron Reagan were made possible through the cooperation of Sharyn P. and Richard Bass, Schick Cattery, Lorton, Virginia: title page, pages 21, 37, 44, 58, 61, 88, 100, 101, 104, 105, 108, 109, 110, 112 (bottom), 116-17, 124 (bottom), 125, 133, 137, 148, 153, and 155.

1996 Edition

9 8 7 6 5 4 3 2   95 789

Distributed in the UNITED STATES to the Pet Trade by T.F.H. Publications, Inc., One T.F.H. Plaza, Neptune City, NJ 07753; distributed in the UNITED STATES to the Bookstore and Library Trade by National Book Network, Inc. 4720 Boston Way, Lanham MD 20706; in CANADA to the Pet Trade by H & L Pet Supplies Inc., 27 Kingston Crescent, Kitchener, Ontario N2B 2T6; Rolf C. Hagen Ltd., 3225 Sartelon Street, Montreal 382 Quebec; in CANADA to the Book Trade by Vanwell Publishing Ltd., 1 Northrup Crescent, St. Catharines, Ontario L2M 6P5 ; in ENGLAND by T.F.H. Publications, PO Box 15, Waterlooville PO7 6BQ; in AUSTRALIA AND THE SOUTH PACIFIC by T.F.H. (Australia), Pty. Ltd., Box 149, Brookvale 2100 N.S.W., Australia; in NEW ZEALAND by Brooklands Aquarium Ltd. 5 McGiven Drive, New Plymouth, RD1 New Zealand; in Japan by T.F.H. Publications, Japan—Jiro Tsuda, 10-12-3 Ohjidai, Sakura, Chiba 285, Japan; in SOUTH AFRICA by Lopis (Pty) Ltd., P.O. Box 39127, Booysens, 2016, Johannesburg, South Africa. Published by T.F.H. Publications, Inc.

MANUFACTURED IN THE UNITED STATES OF AMERICA
BY T.F.H. PUBLICATIONS, INC.

This is the
Maine Coon Cat

By Sharyn P. Bass

Dedication

This book is dedicated to the memory of *James E. Swart, D.V.M.*, for his faithful and loving concern for all living creatures.

Acknowledgments

Grateful appreciation is extended to:

Pat and Chet Howard for their assistance in the development of Schick Cattery.

John M. Duszak, D.V.M., Richmond, Virginia, for his assistance with the medical information contained herein.

My wonderful family—Richard, Cheryl and Jason Bass—for their support of my endeavors.

Carol A. Kyle, editor, for her encouragement and enthusiasm.

And last, but certainly not least, Maine Coon Cats everywhere!

About the Author

Sharyn P. Bass has been a Maine Coon Cat breeder under the name of Schick Cattery since 1977. She is employed by a law firm located in Springfield, Virginia, but devotes much of her spare time to animal welfare. Mrs. Bass is the mother of two children: Cheryl, age 12, and Jason, age 2.

Left to right: Cheryl, Richard, Jason, and Sharyn Bass. Photo: Louise A. Peterson.

Contents

History and Development of the Maine Coon Cat

MYSTERIOUS ORIGINS

There is a great deal of folklore and mystery surrounding the origin of the Maine Coon Cat. Many tales have been passed down through the centuries concerning the breed's ancestors and origin.

Many people believe that the Maine Coon originated from the interbreeding of the American bobcat or Canadian lynx with domestic cats that were brought to North America by sailors. Although the Maine Coon closely resembles the bobcat, because both cats have tufts of hair on the ears and a ruff around the neck, the possibility of a bobcat origin for the Maine Coon is highly unlikely. There are, however, a great number of people who believe in it and are still trying to find proof for their case.

Another mistaken belief is that the domestic cats in New England bred with raccoons, hence the name "Maine Coon Cat." Perhaps the rings on the tabby Maine Coon's tail aided this belief. The breeding of the bobcat and the domestic cat is considered genetically impossible; even more so is the breeding of the domestic cat and the raccoon. At least the concept of the bobcat as a Maine Coon ancestor keeps the origin in the feline family!

One of the more colorful bits of folklore surrounding this breed is that the Maine Coon is the descendant of

Maine Coon Cats are a naturally healthy, hardy breed whose ancestors hailed from New England. Today, these beautiful felines are bred in all parts of the United States. Ch. Patchet's Samantha of Schick. Breeders: Pat and Chet Howard. Owners: Sharyn and Richard Bass. Photo: Sharyn Bass.

the cats which at one time belonged to the French queen Marie Antoinette. During the French Revolution, the queen found that her life was in grave danger and shipped many of her worldly goods, including her six beloved cats, to this country on a ship owned by Captain Clough. The queen herself never made the journey to join them, however, for she was beheaded before her planned escape. It is said that some of the queen's furniture is still to be found in Wiscassett, Maine, which may lend some credence to the account. It's assumed that the queen's cats bred with the American cats—and such was the origin of the Maine Coon.

The most logical explanation, although not quite so colorful, is that the Maine Coon Cat developed naturally over the centuries, due to matings between shorthaired and longhaired cats. The shorthaired cats were brought over by the Pilgrims to kill mice on the ships and on the farms. Later, longhaired beauties were brought over when the appeal for longhaired pets increased. Recent breeding of these two varieties has produced a coat type similar to that of our Maine Coon.

The mystery surrounding the Maine Coon Cat will exist as long as the breed itself does. These tales and the tales surrounding the bravery and prowess of the breed have only served to insure its appeal to all.

A NATURAL BREED

The Maine Coon Cat is America's only natural breed of domestic feline. A natural breed is one which nature alone has created over the years. Most natural breeds of animals are much healthier than domestic animals. When animals are allowed to breed in the wild, without the intervention of man, the process naturally culls out the undesirable weaknesses and accentuates the points that are necessary for survival.

Man did not interfere with the development of the Maine Coon with the process of selective breeding; only the most intelligent "forest-wise" cats and those with physical attributes which enabled them to last in the wild would be expected to survive. As in all of nature, only the best-adapted will live to breed again in the next season. The weak, underdeveloped and unintelligent will not survive. This cycle has been repeated for generations of Maine Coon Cats, and evolution itself has disposed of the poorly equipped and unhealthy. Succeeding generations have carried on only the necessary characteristics for survival.

The New England climate is extremely cold; the terrain is rough and rugged. Any animal surviving in a climate such as this must also be rugged. For the Maine Coon to have existed in this harsh environment, many physical changes must have occurred subsequent to its original form, while many of its original positive features must have been reinforced. Remember that the conditions under which the Maine Coon developed consisted of an untamed land, with few houses for protection and certainly no electricity for warmth.

The Maine Coon's coat developed over the centuries into one of efficient protection against the elements of New England. The short hair on the shoulders, which only gradually gets longer on the back and sides, enables the cat to move through wooded areas without becoming entangled in trees and brambles. If the Maine Coon's coat had been the texture and length of the Persian's, for example, it could have easily been trapped in the briars and woods. Unable to escape, it would have met certain death from starvation or larger predators.

The hair on the back and sides of the Maine Coon is called "guard hair"; it is fairly stiff to the touch. This serves as added insulation to keep the cat warm and dry, just as feathers do on a bird.

The hairs on the stomach, britches, and ruff around the face are much softer than the guard hairs on the back and sides. This soft coat on the stomach enables the cat to lie on soft snow without sinking into it, while at the same time provides necessary warmth and helps retain body heat. Although the hair on the stomach is longer than the rest of the coat, it is not so long as to tangle or mat with snow and ice as the animal walks through the huge snowdrifts of New England.

The ears of the Maine Coon are very distinctive. The long tufts of hair do more than keep the ears warm. Much of the breed's survival in past years depended upon excellent hearing, and the large, tufted ears permit better hearing ability from all directions. Maine Coons

The dark rings on the bushy tail of this brown mackerel patched tabby, together with its ability to sit up on its haunches, may have led to the myth that Maine Coons evolved from feline/raccoon matings. This, of course, is genetically impossible! Shy Precious of Schick. Breeder: Arlene Rodgers. Owners: Sharyn and Richard Bass. Photo: Sharyn Bass.

have the ability to position their ears at many angles in order to distinguish the direction from which a noise is emanating—another factor which helped them to survive. This must have helped the Maine Coon to make a speedy escape to safety when necessary.

The large feet and thick tufts of hair growing between the paw pads act as snowshoes, and better distribute the weight of the cat evenly over a larger area. This characteristic of its development was essential to enable the cat to walk on the icy and snow-covered ground.

The tail of the Maine Coon Cat is one of its loveliest features—yet, once again, nature has determined that even a beautiful tail serves an important and necessary function in the survival of the animal. When the Maine Coon lies down on the cold ground, it wraps this huge bundle of fluff around its body for added protection from the elements. (Foxes and other animals with the same type of tail will also curl it around themselves in bad weather.) When the cat sits, the tail, because of its fluffiness, lies gracefully on top of the snow; it does not sink. The tail also serves as a rudder to help the cat coordinate its movements and make sharp, swift turns.

The coat and the ruff of individual Maine Coons today vary somewhat depending on bloodline and environment. It has been noted that tabbies sometimes have a larger ruff than Maine Coons of other colors, such as solid-colored cats. Perhaps this is because the majority of Maine Coons of long ago were primarily tabbies. The striped tabby coat is believed to be the original Maine Coon color, although this has not been proven. The tabby-colored cats seem to have a greater amount of undercoat, or soft hair, under the guard hairs. Because of the tabby undercoat and the slight harshness of the guard hairs, the tabby's coat seems to stand out more where it is longer, thus giving added fullness.

The eyes of the Maine Coon Cat are green, gold, or copper; white cats are bred with blue or odd-eyed color. If you decide to show your Maine Coon, you will be told that the eye color should complement the coat color, but any color on a Maine Coon is lovely. As with all cats, their ability to see in dimness is excellent, and eye color has nothing to do with the cat's vision.

AMERICA'S FIRST SHOW CAT

The early settlers in New England kept Maine Coons to control the rodent population which spoiled their grain and other crops. It was to be expected that these intelligent cats would find their way into the settlers' homes and become dearly loved pets, as well as good workers.

At least by the 1860's, the farmers, when they gathered to pass the time, would often tell stories about the prowess and abilities of their favorite Maine Coons. The breed, at this time, was developed to the peak of perfection in all areas, including intelligence.

It was during this decade that these farmers began having their own annual cat show at the Skowhegan Fair. There, Maine Coons from all over the territory vied for the coveted title of "Maine State Champion Coon Cat," and interest in the cats flourished.

This thought leads to a very relevant fact; the first cat show in this country generally is believed to have been the Madison Square Garden Cat Show of 1895; however, Maine Coons had been shown at cat shows in New England for some 35 years prior to that date. Our very own beloved breed of American Maine Coon was actually the *first* show cat in America—and rightfully so. How very deserving our Maine Coons are of the title "first show cats in America!"

In 1861, *The Book of the Cat,* by F. R. Pierce, stated that Mr. Pierce owned a Maine Coon by the name of "Captain Jenks of the Horse Marines." Also, in 1895 at a show in New York City, a Maine Coon named Leo was given the honor of Best Cat, followed by a flurry of winnings, only to finally lose to his son in 1900. Surely such written proof of the Maine Coon's popularity at this time tends to point out that it was America's first show cat. Another interesting fact is that the first volume of the Cat Fanciers' Association register contains 28 Maine Coons consisting of a variety of colors. The Maine Coon Cat was *finally,* after all this time, accepted by the Cat

Fanciers' Association for championship status and showing in 1976.

Longhaired cats with pedigrees came into great favor in America at the turn of the century, and our Maine Coons began to decrease in popularity and disappear from the shows. This period of time was very hard for the breed, which was still loved and revered (as both workers and pets) by many New Englanders. Many Maine Coons had been neutered by this time (as it was common for many small farmers to do this for economic reasons), and by 1904, Maine Coons had all but disappeared from the cat shows in America. Thus, our beautiful Maine Coons, which had helped to tame a wild land and had once been much honored, were almost extinct.

Many concerned people who loved Maine Coons and wanted to see them restored to their rightful place of dignity formed the Central Maine Cat Club in 1953. This club arranged shows consisting of only Maine Coons. By the 1960's, the Maine Coon was struggling to make a comeback with the help of many such admirers. These loyal patrons established the Maine Coon Breeders and Fanciers Association in 1968; this association still remains as a national overseer of the welfare of the breed. After a great deal of hard work by many people, the Maine Coon has finally been accepted for championship status in all cat registering organizations in America.

The Maine Coon, America's first show cat and only natural breed of domestic cat, fell from grace only to make a remarkable, but slow, comeback into the hearts of American cat lovers. The breed will certainly enjoy the distinction it deserves as long as cat shows exist, and cat lovers exist. The Maine Coon Cat still remains one of the most exciting and interesting breeds of domestic felines anywhere!

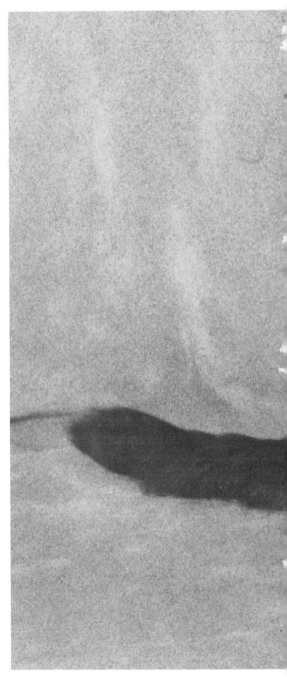

In his full winter coat, showing excellent ear tufts and ruff, is Ch. Sergeant Whiskers of Schick. Owners: Sharyn and Richard Bass. Photo: Sharyn Bass.

17

Appearance and Personality of the Maine Coon Cat

GROWTH AND DEVELOPMENT

Maine Coon kittens are very much like any other kittens, with a few exceptions. They are very hardy, and seldom will a breeder lose a Maine Coon kitten. The kittens' ability to survive and flourish is due to the fact that they are a natural breed and man has not had ample time in which to destroy what nature has intended for the Maine Coon. Unlike many other breeds, such as Persians, Siamese, and others, the Maine Coon Cat has not been "tampered with" to any great extent; therefore, the breed still remains pure and as nature developed it.

Many Persians now have respiratory problems because of their snub noses, which came about in recent years because judges and breeders preferred a flat face. Siamese cats have been bred and inbred for such fine bones and length of head that perhaps in time they will suffer from weakness in those parts. Contrary to these breeding practices, the Maine Coon has not been so physically altered and can be expected to remain very hardy and healthy for some time to come.

Although there are exceptions because of differences of bloodlines, most Maine Coon kittens begin walking, climbing, and sometimes opening their eyes a bit sooner than the kittens of other breeds. They grow at a remarkable rate of speed and are usually fairly large kittens by

Maine Coon kittens are balls of fluff. Later, they lose their fluffy, kitten coats and develop the heavy, shaggy adult coats for which they are known. Pictured is four-week old Schick's Spittin' Image, a brown mackerel tabby female. Breeders/owners: Sharyn and Richard Bass. Photo: Sharyn Bass.

the age of four to eight months. However, this fast growth sometimes slows down at around one year, and in many bloodlines, individuals do not fully develop until they are three to five years old.

Maine Coon kittens will lose their fluffy, kitten coats which later will be replaced with a harsher, adult coat. Although some kittens look quite gangly at this stage of development, don't let this fool you for a minute into thinking the kitten will look that way forever. When the new coat grows in, your Maine Coon will be even more beautiful than imagined.

Full bone development is usually reached around two years of age, again depending upon bloodlines. The Maine Coon in most instances, however, continues to mature for quite a while beyond this age by adding muscle tone and weight. There is no definite point at which we can say the cat will be completely full-grown.

19

Ch. Patchet's Mokie Mudpie of Schick, a black-and-white bi-color male. Breeders: Pat and Chet Howard. Owners: Sharyn and Richard Bass. Photo: Sharyn Bass.

Maine Coon studs will sometimes become so enthralled with the opposite sex that they will not eat what is necessary for proper growth and this, to the consternation of many breeders, will slow a stud's growth rate considerably. This is especially true if a male is used at stud before his growth potential is reached. Using a stud too often will sometimes cause a male, who should be a rather hefty fellow, to remain a lightweight. By limiting the use of the stud, he will once again begin to put on weight and develop properly.

There has been a great deal of discussion concerning just how large today's Maine Coon Cat can and should be in relation to its ancestors. People seem to be very size conscious when it comes to this breed of feline—as if "bigger" were "better." Often, judges at cat shows will not put up a cat for wins because of lack of size, although the type and conformation of the cat may be good. This is unfair, because type in this breed should be given the same attention as weight. That large cat you see is not necessarily a Maine Coon—some Siamese neuters can become really hefty fellows, too! Therefore, unless the cat has the distinctive characteristics of the Maine Coon, such as a bushy tail, tufted ears, a ruff, and a shaggy coat, that larger cat with considerably less type should not be put up for wins either. Both size *and* type must go hand-in-hand, for either characteristic without the other defeats the purpose of the show Standard, which is perfection.

The belief that Maine Coon Cats should weigh between 30 and 40 pounds, as reportedly they did long ago, is stretching the imagination. Perhaps when the cats were in a natural environment they did weigh close to those limits—but certainly not now. The Maine Coon in a wild, rugged land needed to grow as large as possible in order to survive, but for today's pet, it is not necessary. Remember that, genetically speaking, it is much easier to lose size than to gain it.

All Maine Coons are not unusually large felines as many people believe. The beautiful, thick coat of this Maine Coon makes the cat appear larger than it really is. Photo: Ron Reagan.

Many would like to think of the Maine Coon as being the largest domestic feline, both at the present time and historically. However, this has never been proven and probably never will be because of the individuality of bloodlines and lack of substantiation of the size of early Maine Coons. Only occasionally do we see individuals of more than 15 pounds. The weight of most males ranges from 10 to 15 pounds; as in most breeds, a neutered male seems to reach a larger size than a whole male. Most females range in weight from about seven to 10 pounds. These are the *average* weights for the breed as a whole.

In order for the Maine Coon Cat to achieve its rightful place in the show and pet world, it is very important for pet owners, spectators, exhibitors and judges to realize that the Maine Coon is not a *gigantic* cat compared with other large breeds—but rather only a *large* breed of cat.

Those who have never seen one, but have read about them, believe the Maine Coon should be a "super giant" of catdom. This is a misconception that was nurtured through many articles and secondhand stories about the breed. The Maine Coon will more than likely be about the same size as any other large breed of domestic cat, such as the Persian or Himalayan. Cats larger than that are "super giants" and they are few and far between.

Size is also thought somehow to be related to color. For example, A.C. Jude notes in *Cat Genetics* (T.F.H. Publications, Inc., 1977, p.80):

> ". . . the presence of a 'silver' gene
> has effect for smaller size, as noted
> in silver tabby, chinchilla, and
> (probably) the Siamese . . . the
> 'brown' gene tends to an increase
> in size."

When this is recognized by more people in the cat world, the Maine Coon will be accepting even more trophies for Best Cat in Show. After all, it is the total cat which must always be considered—type and quality should always be considered equal, if not preferable, to mere size.

The Maine Coon is a giant—not in body—but in heart and spirit!

TEMPERAMENT AND TRAITS

Maine Coon females seem to know instinctively that they are much sought after and each one firmly believes herself to be Scarlett O'Hara reincarnated (although that beauty was definitely not from Maine). As in most breeds, Maine Coon females are somewhat smaller than the males. They carry themselves with great dignity and are most gracious animals. Do not let those feminine wiles fool you though, because when annoyed, they seem to be more vocal than their masculine counterparts. If they are unhappy, they will most assuredly let you know. Although their vocalizing is ordinarily of very low pitch and not unpleasant to the ears, they will not let a complaint go by without calling it to your attention. As in all breeds, a female in season can be very disturbing to one's nerves; however, if she is not to be bred, it is recommended that your female be spayed—thus saving you many sleepless nights!

Maine Coon males have a very quiet tone of voice and generally do not vocalize as much as the females. The males will, however, carry on a conversation with you if they are in the mood for it. A male will sense a female in heat and repeatedly nag to be allowed to visit her. This also can be annoying, and having your male Maine Coon neutered will quiet his urges.

As kittens, Maine Coons, both males and females, will often open their mouths to cry, but no sound will come out. Others chirp like squirrels or chipmunks. Throughout their lives, except when in season, their voices will remain quiet and subdued.

The Maine Coon is very often referred to as the "tail with the cat attached." Maine Coons will sometimes carry their tail straight up in the air but at other times, perhaps when they are unhappy or frightened, they will let it drag behind them, almost to the floor or ground. It is thought by some—but it is not substantiated—that it is the male who most often carries the tail up high and the female who most often carries (or rather "trails") it gracefully behind her.

The Maine Coon, perhaps because of its many years at nature's knife edge, is an extremely intelligent cat. They also love human companionship and attention, although at times they may seem to be somewhat aloof. This aloofness could more correctly be termed "dignity" or "independence."

The Maine Coon is an extremely dignified animal—neither bounding through the house knocking over plants and furniture, nor exhibiting the desire to climb up your expensive draperies. As kittens, they will certainly try the same mischievous escapades as would any other kitten. However, once maturity is reached, they will usually be quite content to sit and observe everything in a quiet, supervisory manner.

Maine Coons are not to be termed "sissies," however. Just as the female seems to realize her beauty and to luxuriate in it, the male recognizes his masculinity. Maine Coon studs could be considered the "macho men" of catdom. They become so self-assured that nothing is too big for them to tackle. Sometimes, to the chagrin of Maine Coon exhibitors, a breeding male will be more than glad to direct some of this *machismo* toward the judges at cat shows. This temporary change in temperament can be quieted somewhat by a respite from stud service and an

Graceful and dignified, these two females seem to exude all that is beautiful about the breed. Ch. Schick's Shendorah Valentine, a tortoiseshell-and-white, pictured in the foreground with her mother Ch. Schick's Beautiful Dreamer, a brown classic patched tabby. Breeders/owners: Sharyn·and Richard Bass. Photo: Sharyn Bass.

Many Maine Coons have the habit of "scooping up" their water in the same way that raccoons do—perhaps another reason that led to the myth about the domestic cat/raccoon cross! Photo: Sharyn Bass.

As pets, Maine Coons are sweet, affectionate, and playful, and they will keep you entertained for hours with their favorite games and tricks. Ch. Patchet's Samantha of Schick. Breeders: Pat and Chet Howard. Owners: Sharyn and Richard Bass. Photo: Sharyn Bass.

extra portion of human companionship. Just as in other breeds, however, there are some Maine Coons who never seem to develop a taste for cat shows—only a taste for judges!

The Maine Coon has some distinct traits which are unknown in other breeds. One type of observed behavior is that they seem to revel in butting, "goat-wise," their owner's head. Most Maine Coons will do this, and once the owner learns the technique of squatting on all fours with his or her head lowered to the ground—that is, once the owner has been "trained"—the cat will really exert itself, especially if the cat believes that the owner enjoys the game! Although the Maine Coon loves to butt heads with its owner, it does not usually do so with other cats, which is somewhat of a mystery, since the animal is certainly big enough to defend itself should the other cat start to take the game seriously.

Another trait of the Maine Coon is to rise up on its hind legs or haunches, whether to eat or to study something interesting. The Maine Coon does this with a great display of balance and will sit in this manner for quite some time. This trait has strengthened the belief that the original Maine Coon was part raccoon, as this behavior is typical of raccoons when eating. Very rarely will cats of other breeds sit up in this fashion, except for those—such as the Siamese—which have a great amount of balance and grace.

On the whole, the Maine Coon is a loving and docile companion and will reward its owner with many years of affection. Although each cat will have its own unique temperament and traits, it will, for the most part, remain loyal to those who love and care for it.

Foundation vs. Pedigreed Stock

There has been some controversy and ill-feeling regarding the question of whether foundation stock Maine Coons should be shown along with pedigreed stock Maine Coons at cat shows. There are a variety of *pros* and *cons* involved and every breeder is entitled to his or her particular opinion.

A cat is of "pedigreed" stock if in its background it has several generations of registered and recorded ancestors. A cat is of "foundation" stock if its ancestors are unknown. Until January, 1983, the Cat Fanciers' Association was the only cat registering organization that allowed foundation Maine Coons to be registered and shown for championship, and they have been shown extensively in CFA over the years since the breed's acceptance by this organization. CFA has closed its books to the registration of foundation cats with unknown ancestors. (All other associations require a Maine Coon to have three to five generations of recorded ancestors before it can be shown.) There is no longer a need for foundation stock, as the gene pool for Maine Coons is more than sufficient in order for breeders to develop the colors and characteristics that they desire.

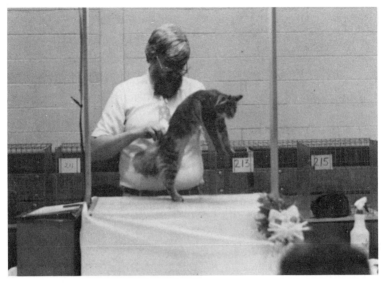

CFA judge Bill Beck examines Tanstaafl's Veronica of Schick, a promising five-month old brown classic patched tabby. Breeders: Mike and Beth Hicks. Owners: Sharyn and Richard Bass. Photo: Sharyn Bass.

Judges at cat shows evaluate each individual cat according to the official Standard of whatever cat association they represent. Each entry (cat) is judged on its own merits, and whether it is of pedigreed or foundation stock makes the cat no better or worse in the eyes of the judges.

Since the Maine Coon is a natural breed, it is obvious that at one time there were no pedigreed Maine Coons in existence. In fact, if one looks into the background of *any* pedigreed animal, it will be obvious that the originals of the breed could not possibly have been pedigreed. However, over a period of time, interested owners began keeping records of their animals' descendants. This record-keeping of ancestors and descendants made such animals pedigreed.

In foundation stock, there is no record of a cat's ancestors available. Yet, should a foundation cat make important wins over a pedigreed cat at shows, the wins are no less valuable. A Maine Coon that is put up at a show for big wins usually deserves it because of its good type or other redeeming features. This is where the controversy arises: should a foundation Maine Coon be shown against pedigreed Maine Coons or be used only in a breeding program? Many owners of pedigreed stock believe foundation cats are not worthy of showing. Owners of foundation stock believe that if the cat fits the Standard and is accepted to be shown, it *should* be shown, whence comes the friction between the two schools of thought.

Since a Standard has been devised and generally agreed upon by a majority of breeders, shouldn't each cat be judged solely upon this Standard of Perfection and not upon the status or non-status of its ancestors? In the author's opinion, it is far better to allow the foundation stock to be shown, to have the individual cat judged according to the Standard, and *then* to judge the cat's descendants, rather than to base an opinion upon its ancestors or lack of them.

A foundation cat that meets the Standard, but which consistently produces undesirable offspring after a few breedings with different mates, should not be bred further or shown, as it carries unwanted genes and, thus, is not a fine representative of the breed. Such a cat, even if it has attained the coveted title of "grand champion," should be dealt with no longer, as it could cause irreparable damage to the breed as a whole, especially in regard to coat type.

If, on the other hand, the line that developed from this foundation cat becomes even *better* than the original cat, it would only hurt the breed as a whole *not* to show it and to continue to improve the individual features set forth in the Standard. This is why judges must learn as much as possible about the Maine Coon and select only those cats that conform to the Standard as closely as possible. After that, its descendants will prove how really good or bad the cat is and whether or not it is worthy of continued breeding.

Also, should a feline registering organization elect to accept foundation stock for showing, then both foundation and pedigreed Maine Coons are entitled to fair competition.

From all indications, breeders of both pedigreed and foundation Maine Coons are genuinely interested in the efforts to better the breed. Many breeders have both pedigreed and foundation stock in their catteries and enjoy showing both equally. Both types of Maine Coons have very good points about them which could be advantageous to the perfection of the breed as a whole. Many foundation cats have excellent ruffs and ear tufts, which may be lacking in some of the pedigreed lines and, likewise, some of the pedigreed cats seem to have a nicer temperament than the foundation cats. However, these are generalizations; much depends on the individual cat.

One advantage of purchasing a pedigreed cat is that one usually can tell from a pedigree, in a general sense, what an unborn cat will look like when it reaches adulthood and how it will reproduce. If one's goal is to establish a good line of Maine Coons, breeding pedigreed cats is a faster means than using foundation stock where one is dealing with unknowns. Good characteristics could be set sooner using pedigreed cats, as well as acquiring knowledge of what faults need to be dealt with. Breeders of pedigreed stock, who have consistency and statistics on their side, do not have some of the problems that face breeders of foundation stock. However, foundation breeders are faced with quite a challenge: to reach the goal of establishing near-perfect Maine Coons by the art of selection in order to make the new line as nearly perfect as possible. Those cats who do not closely meet the Standard must be given away in order to upgrade the new line more quickly.

Ultimately, both types of stock should be utilized in order to perfect the breed. Perhaps in a few years, after the controversy has been settled, all breeders will be working and helping one another for the best interest of the Maine Coon Cat.

SHOW STANDARDS AND ACCEPTED COLORS

The following is the show Standard adopted by the Cat Fanciers' Association, Inc., which is the largest American cat registering organization. The Standard varies somewhat between different registering bodies, but this one gives a good idea of what judges look for and what breeders strive for in the Maine Coon Cat.

POINT SCORE

HEAD (30)
    Shape 15
    Ears 10
    Eyes 5

BODY (35)
    Shape 20
    Neck 5
    Legs and Feet 5
    Tail 5

COAT (20)

COLOR (15)
    Body Color 10
    Eye Color 5

Sup. Gr. Ch. Friscoon's Buffalo Bill, a brown-and-white tabby male is a fine specimen of the breed, as evidenced by his impressive wins, including Tenth Best Cat All-American, 1982; MCBFA's Best Cat, 1982; and TICA's Sixth Best Cat, Second Best Longhair, and Best Maine Coon, 1982. Breeders/owners: Pat Herrmann and Robert Salerno. Photo: Robert Pearcy.

General: Originally a working cat, the Maine Coon is solid, rugged, and can endure a harsh climate. A distinctive characteristic is its smooth, shaggy coat. With an essentially amiable disposition, it has adapted to varied environments.

Head shape: Medium in width and medium long in length with a squareness to the muzzle. Allowance should be made for broadening in older studs. Cheek bones high. Chin firm and in line with nose and upper lip. Nose medium long in length; slight concavity when viewed in profile.

Ears: Large, well-tufted, wide at base, tapering to appear pointed. Set high and well apart.

Eyes: Large, wide set. Slightly oblique setting.

Neck: Medium long.

Body Shape: Muscular, broad-chested. Size medium to large. Females may be smaller than males. The body should be long with all parts in proportion to create a rectangular appearance. Allowance should be made for slow maturation.

Legs and feet: Legs substantial, wide set, of medium length, and in proportion to the body. Paws large, round, well-tufted. Five toes in front; four in back.

Tail: Long, wide at base, and tapering. Fur long and flowing.

Coat: Heavy and shaggy; shorter on the shoulders and longer on the stomach and britches. Frontal ruff desirable. Texture silky with coat falling smoothly.

Penalize: A coat that is short or overall even.

Disqualify: Delicate bone structure. Undershot chin. Crossed eyes. Kinked tail. Incorrect number of toes. Buttons, lockets, or spots.

TICA judge and Maine Coon breeder Beth Hicks shows off Ch. Tanstaafl's Veronica of Schick as a kitten. Sire: Sup. Gr. Ch. Heidi-Ho's Canth of Tanstaafl. Dam: Tanstaafl's Merris Lee. Breeders: Mike and Beth Hicks. Owners: Sharyn and Richard Bass. Photo: Courtesy of the Hicks.

MAINE COON CAT COLORS

Eye color: Eye color should be shades of green, gold, or copper, though white cats may also be either blue or odd-eyed. There is no relationship between eye color and coat color.

SOLID COLOR CLASS

WHITE: Pure glistening white. *Nose Leather and Paw Pads:* Pink.

BLACK: Dense coal black, sound from roots to tip of fur. Free from any tinge of rust on tips or smoke under-coat. *Nose Leather:* Black. *Paw Pads:* Black or Brown.

Longhair finals at cat shows often find a Maine Coon (entry 118) among the winners. Photo: Ron Reagan.

Opposite:
Tortoiseshell-and-white Maine Coons, such as
Ch. Schick's Shendorah Valentine, a female,
are registered in the parti-color classes at
CFA shows. Sire: Ch. Patchet's Mokie Mudpie
of Schick. Dam: Ch. Schick's Beautiful
Dreamer. Breeders/owners: Sharyn and
Richard Bass. Photo: Ron Reagan.

BLUE: One level tone from nose to tip of tail. Sound to the roots. *Nose Leather and Paw Pads:* Blue.

RED: Deep, rich, clear, brilliant red; without shading, markings, or ticking. Lips and chin the same color as coat. *Nose Leather and Paw Pads:* Brick Red.

CREAM: One level shade of buff cream, without markings. Sound to the roots. *Nose Leather and Paw Pads:* Pink.

TABBY COLOR CLASS

CLASSIC TABBY PATTERN: Markings dense, clearly defined and broad. Legs evenly barred with bracelets coming up to meet the body markings. Tail evenly ringed. Several unbroken necklaces on neck and upper chest, the more the better. Frown marks on forehead form an intricate letter '"M." Unbroken line runs back from outer corner of eye. Swirls on cheeks. Vertical lines over back of head extend to shoulder markings which are in the shape of a butterfly with both upper and lower wings distinctly outlined and marked with dots inside outline. Back markings consist of a vertical line down the spine from butterfly to tail with a vertical stripe paralleling it on each side, the three stripes well separated by stripes of the ground color. Large solid blotch on each side to be encircled by one or more unbroken rings. Side markings should be the same on both sides. Double vertical row of buttons on chest and stomach.

MACKEREL TABBY PATTERN: Markings dense, clearly defined and all narrow pencillings. Legs evenly barred with narrow bracelets coming up to meet the body markings. Tail barred. Necklaces on neck and chest distinct, like so many chains. Head barred with an "M" on the forehead. Unbroken lines running back from the eyes. Lines running down the head to meet the shoulders. Spine lines run together to form a narrow saddle. Narrow pencillings run around the body.

SILVER TABBY: Ground color pale, clear silver. Markings dense black. White trim around lip and chin allowed. *Nose Leather:* Brick Red desirable. *Paw Pads:* Black desirable.

RED TABBY: Ground color red. Markings deep, rich red. White trim around lip and chin allowed. *Nose Leather and Paw Pads:* Brick Red desirable.

BROWN TABBY: Ground color brilliant coppery brown. Markings dense black. Back of leg black from paw to heel. White trim around lip and chin allowed. *Nose Leather and Paw Pads:* Black or Brown desirable.

BLUE TABBY: Ground color pale bluish ivory. Markings a very deep blue affording a good contrast with ground color. Warm fawn overtones or patina over the whole. White trim around lip and chin allowed. *Nose Leather:* Old Rose desirable. *Paw Pads:* Rose desirable.

CREAM TABBY: Ground color very pale cream. Markings of buff or cream sufficiently darker than the ground color to afford good contrast but remaining within the dilute range. White trim around lip and chin allowed. *Nose Leather and Paw Pads:* Pink desirable.

CAMEO TABBY: Ground color off-white. Markings red. White trim around lip and chin allowed. *Nose Leather and Paw Pads:* Rose desirable.

PATCHED TABBY PATTERN: A Patched Tabby (Torbie) is an established silver, brown, or blue tabby with patches of red and/or cream.

TABBY WITH WHITE CLASS

TABBY WITH WHITE: Color as defined for Tabby with or without white on the face. Must have white on

TICA judge Marjorie Hanna checks the head shape of this brown tabby male, Sup. Gr. Ch. Heidi-Ho's Canth of Tanstaafl. Owners: Mike and Beth Hicks. Photo: Ron Reagan.

Opposite:
TICA judge Gloria Stephens gives this tabby kitten a final look. Kittens that are between the ages of four and eight months are eligible to be shown in the non-championship classes. Photo: Ron Reagan.

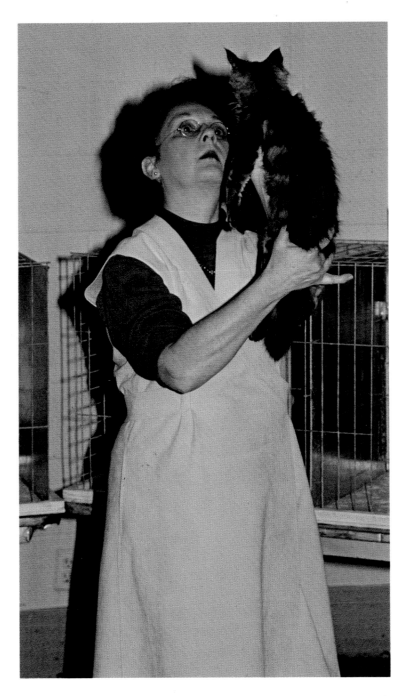

bib, belly, and all four paws. White on one-third of body is desirable. Colors accepted are Silver, Red, Brown, Blue, or Cream.

PATCHED TABBY WITH WHITE (Torbie with White): Color as described for Patched Tabby (Torbie) but with distribution of white markings as described in Tabby with White. Color as described for Patched Tabby (Torbie) with or without white on face. Must have white on bib, belly, and all four paws. White on one-third of body desirable. Colors accepted are Silver, Brown, or Blue.

PARTI-COLOR CLASS

TORTOISESHELL: Black with unbrindled patches of red and cream. Patches clearly defined and well broken on both body and extremities. Blaze of red or cream on face is desirable.

TORTOISESHELL WITH WHITE: Color as defined for Tortoiseshell with or without white on the face. Must have white on bib, belly, and all four paws. White on one-third of body is desirable.

CALICO: White with unbrindled patches of black and red. White predominant on underparts.

DILUTE CALICO: White with unbrindled patches of blue and cream. White predominant on underparts.

BLUE-CREAM: Blue with patches of solid cream. Patches clearly defined and well broken on both body and extremities.

BLUE-CREAM WITH WHITE: Color as defined for Blue-Cream with or without white on the face. Must have white on bib, belly, and all four paws. White on one-third of the body is desirable.

42

BI-COLOR: A combination of a solid color with white. The colored areas predominate with the white portions being located on the face, chest, belly, legs, and feet. Colors accepted are Red, Black, Blue, or Cream.

OTHER MAINE COON COLORS CLASS

CHINCHILLA: Undercoat pure white. Coat on back, flanks, head, and tail sufficiently tipped with black to give the characteristic sparkling silver appearance. Legs may be slightly shaded with tipping. Chin, ear tufts, stomach, and chest, pure white. Rims of eyes, lips, and nose outlined with Black. *Nose Leather:* Brick Red. *Paw Pads:* Black.

SHADED SILVER: Undercoat white with a mantle of black tipping shading down from sides, face, and tail from dark on the ridge to white on the chin, chest, stomach, and under the tail. Legs to be the same tone as the face. The general effect to be much darker than a Chinchilla. Rims of eyes, lips, and nose outlined with Black. *Nose Leather:* Brick Red. *Paw Pads:* Black.

SHELL CAMEO (Red Chinchilla): Undercoat white, the coat on the back, flanks, head, and tail to be sufficiently tipped with red to give the characteristic sparkling appearance. Face and legs may be very slightly shaded with tipping. Chin, ear tufts, stomach, and chest white. *Nose Leather, Rims of Eyes, and Paw Pads:* Rose.

SHADED CAMEO (Red Shaded): Undercoat white with a mantle of red tipping shading down the sides, face, and tail from dark on the ridge to white on the chin, chest, stomach, and under the tail. Legs to be the same tone as face. The general effect to be much redder than the Shell Cameo. *Nose Leather, Rims of Eyes, and Paw Pads:* Rose.

Ch. Schick's Beautiful Dreamer leaving the show hall in a safe cat carrier. Breeders/owners: Sharyn and Richard Bass. Photo: Ron Reagan.

Opposite:
Part of the grooming process when you prepare your Maine Coon for a cat show is to clip its claws. Photo: Ron Reagan.

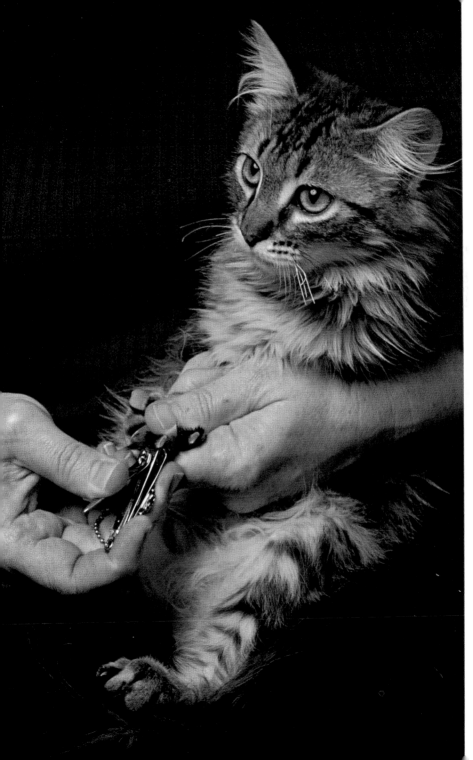

BLACK SMOKE: White undercoat, deeply tipped with black. Cat in repose appears black. In motion the white undercoat is clearly apparent. Points and mask black with narrow band of white at base of hairs next to skin which may be seen only when fur is parted. Light silver frill and ear tufts. *Nose Leather and Paw Pads:* Black.

BLUE SMOKE: White undercoat, deeply tipped with blue. Cat in repose appears blue. In motion the white undercoat is clearly apparent. Points and mask blue with narrow band of white hairs next to skin which may be seen only when fur is parted. White frill and ear tufts. *Nose Leather and Paw Pads:* Blue.

CAMEO SMOKE (Red Smoke): White undercoat, deeply tipped with red. Cat in repose appears red. In motion the white undercoat is clearly apparent. Points and mask red with narrow band of white at base of hairs next to skin which may be seen only when fur is parted. *Nose Leather, Rims of Eyes, and Paw Pads:* Rose.

For comparison purposes, below is the Maine Coon Breeders and Fanciers Association official Standard. MCBFA is a national organization dedicated to "the promotion and protection of the Maine Coon Cat."

General Statement: The Maine Coon is a solid, rugged cat and is America's only natural longhaired breed. Type must not be sacrificed for size or size for type—the optimum being a large typey cat. Females are somewhat smaller than males and allowance should be made for slow maturation of the breed.

Head: Medium in length and width, with a squareness to the muzzle. Allowance should be made for broadening in males. Cheek bones high. Nose medium in length with a gentle concave curve and no break or bump. Chin firm and in line with upper lip and nose.

Eyes: Large, wide set, slightly oblique setting. Eye color can be shades of green, gold, or copper, though white cats may be blue or odd-eyed. There is no relationship between eye color and coat color. Clarity of eye color is desirable.

Ears: Large, wide at base, moderately pointed and well tufted. Set high on head approximately an ear's width apart. Lynx-like tipping desirable.

Body: Muscular, medium to large in size, broadchested. Body is long, with all parts in proportion, creating a rectangular appearance. When viewed from the rear there is a definite squareness to the rump. Neck medium long.

Legs and Paws: Legs substantial, wide set, medium in length, contributing to a rectangular appearance, Paws large, round, well-tufted (5 toes in front, 4 toes in back).

Tail: Long, equal to body in length (distance from end of rump to shoulders), wide at base and tapering. Fur full, long and flowing.

Coat: Fur on shoulders is short, gradually increasing in length along back and sides, ending in full britches and long shaggy belly fur. Fur is soft but has body, falls smoothly, and lies close to the body. A slight undercoat is carried. A full ruff is not expected; however, there should be a frontal ruff beginning at the base of the ears.

Coat Colors: All recognized colors. White trim around the chin and lip permitted except in solid colored cats.

Disqualifications: Buttons, lockets, spots, overall even coat, short cobby body, crossed eyes, kinked tail, incorrect number of toes.

Penalties: Delicate bone structures, untufted paws, poor condition, nose break or bump, undershot chin, short rounded muzzle.

The beautiful plume-like tail is one of the most outstanding Maine Coon features, and it is especially striking on Charmall Animation of Maineberg, a black female. Breeders: James and Virginia Molloy. Owner: Pat Bergman. Photo: Ron Reagan.

Opposite:
Arden's Manitou of Schick, a flashy red mackerel tabby male pictured at eight months of age. Breeder: Carol Knowles. Owners: Sharyn and Richard Bass. Photo: Jan Carson.

Entering a Cat Show

The first cat show a novice exhibitor attends can be a very exciting but confusing event. Excitement runs high, but disappointment also shows its face. Between trying to remember the cat's number, keeping up with the judging schedule, talking to other exhibitors and grooming the cat, the novice can become very frustrated and uncomfortable. However, if one knows what to expect, one can be better prepared to accept the unexpected. Unfortunately, this comes only with experience, and the best way to get experience is to dive in. Cat shows are wonderful places where people meet others with the same common interest. But amid this socializing and chatter, the main thought should be to present your cat in the best possible manner, with the hope that it will go home with many good wins and ribbons to its credit.

In order to win, a Maine Coon must, of course, be capable of winning and be registered with whichever association is sponsoring the show. The cat can be shown at any show given by the organization with which it is registered. In other words, if your cat is registered with the Cat Fanciers' Association, you may enter it in any CFA show in the country. Most people will usually enter the shows which are located closest to their homes—at least until the "show bug" bites them and they begin traveling greater distances to extend their reputation and wins.

At most cat shows, show cages will be provided for the entries. Be sure to thoroughly clean and disinfect the cage in which your Maine Coons will remain until they are ready to be judged. Then add those furnishings that will make your cats feel at home: a litter box, food and water dishes, toys, a rug, and curtains. Photo: Sharyn Bass.

Most cat magazines, such as *Cats* and *Cat Fancy*, list upcoming shows. It is also possible to speak with someone who belongs to a local cat club, as the clubs are usually abreast of the various shows. You could also write to the association that has registered your cat to request show dates in your particular region.

After you have decided which show you would like to enter, you must write to the Entry Clerk of that particular show and request details and entry blanks. The Entry Clerk will send you all the necessary information you will need concerning rules, location, times, and what the club will furnish for the care of your cat. The cage dimensions will be given, and you will need to bring curtains and rugs for your cat's comfort and privacy. Many novice exhibitors use large bath towels for curtains, and

Roselu Rococo of Cat Clan, a brown tabby male. Sire: Tony Boy of Roselu. Dam: Roselu's Lady Godiva. Breeder: Helen M. Wohlfort. Owner: Fay Kinsey. Photo: Ron Reagan. Maine Coons that are destined for the show ring should become accustomed to frequent handling, regular grooming sessions, traveling, and to being confined (for both short and long intervals) in their cat carriers.

Patchet's Good Time Cholly, a brown mackerel tabby male, showing good type and distinct tabby markings. Sire: Ch. Sergeant Whiskers of Schick. Dam: Miss Priss of Patchet. Breeders: Pat and Chet Howard. Owners: Sharyn and Richard Bass. Photo: Sharyn Bass.

clothespins to hold the towels in place; this seems sufficient—after all, it is the *cat* that will be judged, not the cage! Later on you may decide to make fancy curtains which complement the color of your cat.

Also included in the information package sent by the Entry Clerk will be the names of the judges and whether they will be specialty judges (shorthair or longhair only) or all-breed judges (both shorthair and longhair judged against one another for the top ten cats in show). You will also be told the entry closing date, which is usually a few weeks before the show. All entries *must* be received by the closing date, so that catalog listings and other details can be confirmed.

The information you put on the entry blank must be exact and written legibly so that the information will appear correctly in the catalog and judges' books. Should such information be incorrect, any wins your cat makes may be disqualified by the association when it receives the judges' books after the show. It is imperative, therefore, that all information on the entry blank be correct.

The entry blank usually will ask which color class the cat belongs in; if you are not sure, request that the Entry Clerk, who should have all of this information at hand, insert the number of the class for you. In general, should you not understand something or have any problem, and you have no one nearby to explain it, the best procedure would be to telephone the Entry Clerk and ask for assistance.

According to CFA, there are three main categories in which a cat could be entered: non-championship, championship, and premiership. *Non-championship* classes consist of kittens (four to eight months of age) and household pets (non-registered cats with unknown ancestors, and which must be spayed or neutered, usually before eight months). *Championship* classes consist of recognized and registered breeds over the age of eight months that are not neutered or spayed. *Premiership* classes consist of adult cats that have been altered and are of registered breeds. No cat can be shown in any category if it has been declawed.

CFA judge Walter Friend holds up seven-month old Ch. Patchet's Samantha of Schick as he awards her with Fourth Best Longhair Kitten in Show. Breeders: Pat and Chet Howard. Owners: Sharyn and Richard Bass. Photo: Sharyn Bass.

Charmalot Strawberry of Roselu, a red-and-white bi-color female. Sire: Friscoon's Panama Red. Dam: Magnificat's Angeles Bell. Breeders: James and Virginia Molloy. Owner: Helen M. Wohlfort. Photo: Ron Reagan.

Opposite:
Ch. Sergeant Whiskers of Schick, a brown mackerel tabby male. Owners: Sharyn and Richard Bass. Photo: Ron Reagan. Whole (unaltered) cats above the age of eight months that are registered with whatever cat association is sponsoring a particular show are eligible for entry in the championship classes where they may earn points (awards) towards the title of champion (Ch.) and grand champion (Gr. Ch.).

These categories are even further broken down as follows. The championship category is divided into open, champion and grand champion classes. An *open* is a cat which has less than six winner's ribbons and, thus, is not yet a confirmed champion. A *champion* is a cat that has received at least six winner's ribbons, but has not yet defeated the required number of competing champions to become a grand champion. A *grand champion* is a cat that has beaten at least the required number of other champions to gain the title. In CFA shows, the current required number of points for a champion to become a grand champion is 200.

The premiership category is broken down in the same way, such as *open, premier* (which is the equivalent of champion) and *grand premier* (which is the equivalent of

Show cats do not happen by accident; they are the result of a great deal of time and effort. Daily grooming sessions, a well-balanced diet, and lots of human love and attention are all part of preparing your Maine Coon for the big day. The smooth, shiny coat of this beautiful black-and-white bi-color reflects good care. Photo: Ron Reagan.

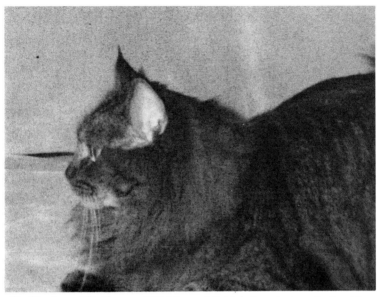

Profile view of Ch. Sergeant Whiskers of Schick. In order to gain the title of Champion, in CFA, he had to win six winner's ribbons. Owners: Sharyn and Richard Bass. Photo: Sharyn Bass.

grand champion, although the number of points needed to reach grand premier may be somewhat fewer than what is required to reach the title of grand champion).

When you send in your completed form to the Entry Clerk, you must include with it a check for the entry fee. Sometimes a discount is given for entries received early or for entering three or more cats—if you have that many cats. This discount is a great help to breeders, as it might otherwise be very expensive to show a number of cats at one time.

You will receive confirmation of your cat's entry, and you will be sent directions to the show hall and information on hotels and motels in the area.

Should motel reservations be necessary, it would be best to make them early. Usually, the show management

Peering out of its own special hideaway is a comfortable, contented Maine Coon. Wicker sleeping baskets such as this, along with a variety of other models, are available in most pet shops. Photo: Ron Reagan.

Opposite above: Ch. Patchet's Mokie Mudpie of Schick, a black-and-white bi-color male. Breeders: Pat and Chet Howard. Owners: Sharyn and Richard Bass. **Opposite below:** Mokie with his daughter Schick's Kabuki, a brown mackerel tabby. Photos: Ron Reagan.

will set aside a number of rooms for exhibitors from out of town; any motel or hotel listed in the confirmation will be certain to accept pets in the rooms (although damages are at the owner's expense). Often, however, these rooms go rather quickly. Other motels and hotels in the vicinity may not accept pets, so it is wise to check this out well in advance of the show.

Once you have sent in your entry blank, have received your confirmation and have made your motel reservations, it is time to concentrate on making your Maine Coon look the best it possibly can. This is the point toward which all of its daily grooming sessions have been directed. To be presentable at a show, a cat should have been cared for daily, given a good diet, exposed to sympathetic human contact, and, in general, prepared for months in order to make its debut with style. A cat cannot become a "show cat" overnight. It takes a myriad of things to complete the picture and make the cat picture-perfect, or rather *show*-perfect.

CAT SHOW PROCEDURES

By the time the show date arrives, you should have received your confirmation of entry, bathed your Maine Coon, clipped its front and back claws, and, in general, you should have your Maine Coon ready for the big event. The procedures for bathing and clipping claws will be more fully covered in the sections on Grooming and Good Health and Grooming for Show.

Before the show, it is best to make a list of all the necessary equipment and supplies you will need to take —especially if you plan to stay overnight. The most important things to remember for the comfort of your cat are the litter box, litter, and food and water from home (very often strange water will upset the cat's digestive system and cause diarrhea). Other necessities include grooming equipment and a sturdy, but comfortable, cat carrier. It may also be wise to take along some people food, too. Many times in the excitement of showing, there is little time to eat except to quickly gulp down a sandwich.

Many cats love to ride in cars, but many get sick from it. It is important that *your* cat be accustomed to traveling. The cat will be more relaxed if you have been putting it in the carrier for short periods of time before the trip to the show and taking it with you in the car whenever possible. It is always best to help the cat adjust gradually to being confined in a carrier and traveling on a long car trip.

Barring any unforeseen incidents, you should arrive at the show hall by the requested check-in time. The first thing to do is to check in with the Entry Clerk, who will give you a card telling you where you are benched (which numbered cage your cat will be spending its time in). Usually, you will also receive a cardboard litter box and dishes for food and water.

Catalogs are available when you check in with the Entry Clerk, or shortly afterwards. They cost a few dollars, but they are indispensable.

It is very important to read the catalog information on your Maine Coon as soon as possible. Be sure to check the cat's registration number against the one in the catalog, and also the rest of the information such as dam, sire, birthdate and class, being sure that all spellings and dates are correct. This information *must* be accurate or, as previously stated, your wins at the show can be disqualified. If there is any error in the printed information, take the catalog to the Master Clerk (who is in charge of sending the catalog with marked wins to the registration association) and point out the errors. This should be done *immediately* upon finding any mistake. You then

TICA judge Pat Smith checks for length of body on Mladia Galadriel, a patched tabby (also known as a torbie). Breeder/owner: Maria Mladjen. Judges use an official standard of perfection as a guideline when evaluating each of the entries they handle; however, their own good judgment and esthetic taste also help them form their decisions in the show ring. Photo: Ron Reagan.

may be asked to inform each of the judges' clerks of the corrections. It is important to see that each judging book has been corrected before you put your cat in the ring.

When you arrive at your numbered cage, the first thing to do is to wipe the cage out with a non-toxic disinfectant. Then set up your curtains and rugs. After the cage is properly cleaned and set up, and the litter box and dishes are installed, it is time to take your Maine Coon out of the carrier and introduce it to its home-away-from-home. The cat will soon settle down and learn to enjoy all of the fuss and attention.

Check the judging schedule for each ring listed. If the Maine Coon cats are listed near the top of the schedule, don't hesitate; it is time to begin grooming. It will be easier to tell when your cat will be called after you become more acquainted with showing. The best advice for a novice is: "Be Prepared."

After a short welcome to exhibitors, the announcer will read the list of absentees. It is very important to remain quiet and pay attention at this time. Usually there is a list in the catalog with each number entered individually so that exhibitors quickly can check off the number of each cat absent.

Whatever you do, don't forget your cat's assigned number (which is listed in the catalog and on your cage). When the time arrives, the announcer will call your cat's number and tell you in which ring your Maine Coon will be judged. However, if there are only a few Maine Coons, the announcer may only say something like, "All Maine Coons to Ring 4." Immediately go to the specified ring. Only three calls of your number will be made and if your cat is not in the ring by the third call, it will be marked absent, and hence disqualified, and judging will continue without your entry.

It is hoped that your Maine Coon has been groomed to perfection and is ready to delight the judges. After placing your entry in the judging ring cage, which has the assigned number on it, give your cat a few extra loving pats and words of confidence, and have a seat in front of the judge. The big moment has finally arrived.

After disinfecting his or her hands and the judging table, the judge will take your cat out of its cage and place it on the table before him or her. The judge will hold the cat up to check for length of body, stand the cat on its hind legs, check the length of the tail and the structure of the head. Using experienced hands and eyes, he or she will check for shape, size, color and texture. After the judge arrives at a decision, he or she will place the cat back in the cage, disinfect his or her hands and table again, and remove the next cat to be judged. Do not remove your cat from the ring at this time unless the Clerk takes your cat's number down or says that it may go back.

Once all of the cats in a color class (solid colors, tabbies, etc.) are judged, the judge will give out the ribbons —First, Second and Third; Best and Second Best of Color; and Winners (red, white and blue). (Remember that it takes six winner's ribbons to make a champion.) The judge will then move to another color class and repeat the procedure. After all of the Maine Coons have been judged for Best of Color wins, the judge will select the Best Champion and Second Best Champion. Then the Best of Breed and Second Best of Breed will be selected. The most a Maine Coon can expect to win at this time is the Best of Breed ribbon.

Remember that each judge will see *every* cat in the show, and it must be very difficult to finally select the Best Cat in Show. Also, each ring in itself is considered to be a separate show and a cat that wins Best of Breed or even Best Cat in Show in one ring may not receive

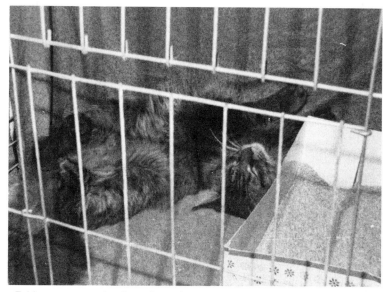

Taking a snooze at a show. Sometimes cardboard litter boxes are provided by the show-giving club for your Maine Coon's comfort. Photo: Sharyn Bass.

anything in the following ring. Therefore, it is possible to have four different Best Cat in Show winners at one cat show. Each ring will, at the close of the show, finally have a Best Cat in Show winner, in addition to awards for Second through Tenth Best Cat.

If your cat is lucky enough to receive a Best of Breed win in a particular ring, it will stand a chance to be among the top ten winning cats at the end of all judging. However, it must be remembered that for a Maine Coon to make the top ten cats, it must defeat a myriad of Persians, Himalayans, and others. Considering the number of entries of these breeds being shown in some associations, it is quite a feat for a Maine Coon to make the top ten.

The judge selects his or her top ten cats from all of the Best of Breed winners which have been judged. Sometimes, if he or she particularly likes two cats of the same breed, he or she may even select Best *and* Second Best of Breed for the top ten cats. It is not unusual to see as many as six or more Persians or Himalayans in the top ten finals.

Do not under any circumstances, however, leave the show hall if you have a Best of Breed win, unless you are absolutely certain your cat could not possibly be among the top ten cats selected. Many exhibitors have left the show early to start a long drive home, only to discover later that their cat would have been in the top ten had they stayed for the finals. What a shame it would be to lose such a glorious win after taking the time and going to the expense of entering the show! Have faith in yourself and in your potential champion.

Remember that throughout the judging, it is both in poor taste and *against the show rules* to speak to any judge unless in response to a question to you or to the handler of the cat. The only time it is proper to speak with the judge is *after* the entire show, perhaps to offer thanks for putting your beautiful Maine Coon in the finals for the top ten cats.

In summary:

DO

...send in your entry form—written legibly—well before the closing date.

...disinfect your cat's cage when you arrive at the show hall.

...make your cat comfortable with fresh water and food and a litter box.

...remember your cat's number so that when it is called you can take it immediately to the judging ring—and not alienate the judge (and the other exhibitors) by making everyone wait.

...remove your cat promptly from the ring after its number is turned down or the clerk says it may be taken back.

. . .try to remain calm no matter what may arise. If you don't, your cat will sense this and be even more frightened and upset.

DON'T

. . .hesitate to check the catalog for your cat's correct entry information as soon as you arrive.

. . .touch or feed a cat not belonging to you, without the owner's express permission. Even so, you are taking a chance of passing germs from one cat to another. On occasion, when cats (especially males) smell the scent of another cat on your hands, they may bite or, at the very least, become too upset to show.

. . .fail to listen to the judges' comments. Many judges remark on a cat's good and bad points and this early education is essential to all exhibitors.

. . .speak to the judge until after the final judging is over.

. . .neglect to thank the judge, if you are lucky enough to have a Maine Coon in the top ten finals.

. . .FORGET TO RELAX AND ENJOY YOURSELF!

Danger Ahead!

There are many dangers lying in wait for the unsuspecting Maine Coon who is unfortunate enough to have a negligent owner. The controversy about whether a feline should be kept inside or allowed its freedom outside is still raging, and will probably continue as long as there is one cat still living. Although there are quite a few dangers outside, there are just as many existing inside the home itself; the difference is that you have more control over what happens indoors.

Most of the dangers outside are evident. Your cat could be injured or killed by an automobile, dog, or another cat. How very painful it must be to find a beloved pet injured or mutilated beyond recovery—not to mention the veterinary bill incurred in trying to save its waning life. The fact that this may happen to a pet at any time if it is allowed out-of-doors must be recognized before the decision is made to allow it outside freedom.

What most cat owners do not realize is that the animal is healthier—and perhaps happier—if kept in the house. If a kitten is kept indoors from the time it is first brought home, it will have no desire to go outside at all, for to this home-raised cat, the outside world is dangerous and suspicious. (How very perceptive of the indoor cat!) On the other hand, a cat that is allowed outdoors occasionally will object to not being allowed out when it feels like it. Therefore, even when you would rather have the cat

There are a number of plants and flowers that are harmful to cats. If you love houseplants, check with your veterinarian or with a local garden center to find out which plants are dangerous to keep around. (See also the list at the end of this chapter.) Photo: Sharyn Bass.

remain inside, the cat that has been allowed outside previously will scurry past you the first time the door is open. And, it will not return until it feels like it. Although you may be leaving shortly for vacation, or there is a bad storm approaching, or your cat happens to be pregnant, it will nevertheless run outside, unmindful of your plans, or nature's. This type of situation can cause a great number of problems, especially to a pregnant cat having her first litter.

Another danger outside the home includes poisoning, which happens much more frequently than we would like to believe. There is always the danger of the cat getting something caustic on its feet and then licking it off while grooming itself. The Maine Coon is especially susceptible to this type of poisoning because of the long tufts of hair on its feet which readily absorb the caustic. A cat walking on a driveway or street certainly will not walk around a few drops of spilled gasoline or oil from an automobile. When the cat decides to clean itself, the feet are also cleaned, and the cat ingests the harmful caustic material which, in sufficient amounts, can cause extreme illness or perhaps death.

Although it would be foolish not to immediately recognize the dangers a dog represents to a cat, many people do not realize the danger one cat may represent to another. The male Maine Coon, particularly, being so "macho," is determined to vigorously protect his territory from other intruding males. Anyone having heard the bellowing and outrageous cries of two males fighting would agree that this should be avoided at all costs. And if the sounds of a cat fight are not bad enough, the injuries that can be sustained are even more horrifying. Two males will fight in a most ungentlemanly fashion—tearing ears, gouging eyes and often mutilating testicles. A cat can be permanently damaged or killed in a matter of minutes. If he is lucky, he may be able to make it home, but the horror you face when you look at your dear pet will never be forgotten. The veterinary bill will, once again, soar and euthanasia may be the only way to save your Maine Coon from a slow and suffering death.

Should you choose to let your pet roam freely outdoors, you must be prepared to accept the consequences of your decision. Besides what has been mentioned above, there are numerous other things that might befall your pet. Your cat will be out of your sight; danger may suddenly arise and how would you possibly know (in time to save its life) that your pet was in mortal danger? Even the problem of fleas and ticks sometimes can be quite challenging.

There are also dangers inside the home that should be recognized. The things you need to watch for when you bring a kitten home are much the same as if you had a small toddler in your home. Although a baby could possibly insert a small toy into a light socket, a kitten could chew the light cord and be electrocuted.

Also, just as a baby should not be allowed beneath a stove with boiling water or food on top of it, neither should a kitten be allowed beneath your feet while you are cooking. Either a child or cat could be scalded if hot liquid were to drop from the stove onto them. Care also must be taken that your cat does not trip you while you carry hot foods. Although your cat may brush against your feet to love you, it doesn't realize the potential dangers this poses to both of you. Cabinets containing cleaning fluids and other caustics should be kept tightly closed so harmful chemicals are beyond the reach of either young humans or young animals.

Flowers and plants in and around the home sometimes can cause illness or possibly death. Although many outside plants are harmful (such as marigolds, poison ivy and rhubarb leaves), the urge to eat greenery is doubled to a cat or kitten kept inside compared to that of an outside cat. This is because the indoor cat does not have grasses to eat which help to clean out its system. Many cats need to eat greens and instinctively will do so, whether they are kept inside or out. Unless a suitable substitute such as oats or fresh, clean grass which is free of pesticides is supplied, a cat invariably will play with and nip at various houseplants.

These are a few of the houseplants that can cause severe illness or death, depending on the amounts ingested:

Plant	Immediate Symptoms	Result
English and Baltic Ivy	Diarrhea	Coma
Philodendron	Swelling of the mouth and throat, blocking windpipe	Death
Dieffenbachia (Dumb Cane)	Swelling of the throat, vomiting, diarrhea	Death
Poinsettia	Blisters on skin, vomiting, irritation, and diarrhea	Death
Mistletoe	Vomiting, diarrhea, convulsions	Coma
Potato (Unripe) or Sprouts	Vomiting, diarrhea	Coma

Since there are many other household plants that can cause illness, it is safest to keep kitty away from *all* plants, if possible. If your home contains any of the above plants, it would be far preferable to remove them to rooms where your cat is not allowed. If there is no place where you can keep these plants away from the cat, it is best to give the plants to a friend without any pets.

Another problem may arise if and when you decide to go on vacation and cannot take your Maine Coon with you. Many cats are upset and frightened when left with a stranger and will immediately find an out-of-the-way place to hide in, such as an unfinished basement or attic. Many times a cat will be so terrified in a strange place that it will remain in such a hideout—resisting food, water, and a litter box—for as long as it can survive.

Perhaps even as much as three weeks later, a dehydrated, starving cat may eventually be found. Many of these animals are found dead, but there are a few that have lived through such an ordeal, just barely clinging to a thread of life. It is always best to either completely check your friend's home for possible dangers before leaving your pet there, or to take your cat to a veterinarian or boarding cattery. The cat may not eat for a few days, but at least it will be safe and have medical care until your return.

Guard your Maine Coon's life as you would that of a child, always considering that there are dangers to be found everywhere. Even the danger of your beautiful pet being stolen is not unlikely. Every year many animals are stolen—either for profit or possible experimentation. Much suffering, both by you and your pet, can be avoided by using common sense and being alert to your cat's needs and requirements. Your home should be made as danger-free as possible. With a little forethought and a great deal of common sense, your pet will live to enjoy its years with you in a safe and happy home.

Maine Coon Care
and Management

The Maine Coon Cat, like most other breeds, needs very few accessories in order to live a happy and healthy life. There are, however, a few essentials that your pet cannot do without, and it is best to have all of the necessities on hand before you bring your new Maine Coon home. The equipment listed below, and a great variety of other items, can be found in most pet shops.

THE LITTER BOX

Litter boxes (or pans) come in a variety of sizes, shapes, and price ranges, and surely there is one to fit the needs of even the most fastidious of felines. Most cats will readily accept the uncovered styles, but many owners prefer their cats to use the completely covered models that are constructed to reduce the scattering of cat litter on the floor. (Scattering of litter occurs, incidentally, whenever a cat attempts to bury its droppings. Cats are very fussy about keeping their litter boxes clean!) Some styles contain charcoal filters or special additives which are designed to absorb and reduce odors.

Whatever type of litter box you choose, be sure to thoroughly clean it *at least* once a week (more often if many cats are using it). Keep in mind that if you keep a dirty litter box around, your Maine Coon may refuse to

Most commercially available brands of cat litter are made of absorbent granulated clay or a similarly absorbent material. Photo courtesy of Hagen.

use it, and instead, will find another spot to deposit its wastes. Discard the soiled litter material and wash the box with hot water and mild detergent. Occasionally, use a disinfectant solution or spray to remove harsh odors and to kill any germs that might be harbored in the litter box. Rinse the box well so as to remove any residue from the disinfectant, and dry the container thoroughly before placing litter in it. Remember that disinfectants (such as bleach) can be very harmful to you and your pet, so extreme care must be taken when using any of these products.

LITTER MATERIAL

While shredded newspaper is an inexpensive and convenient type of litter, it does not absorb a cat's excrements very well, nor does it control odors; therefore, it is not recommended. Commercially prepared litter box fillers, many of which can be found at your local pet shop, are highly recommended. Some litters even contain special odor-absorbing additives, but be advised that some cats—and Maine Coons are no exception—may be repelled by the smell of these scented granules. Check with the person from whom you bought your pet to find out what type of litter the cat or kitten has been accustomed to. Continue using whatever this person recommends; then, if you prefer to use another kind of litter, each time you clean the litter box and change the litter material, gradually add the new material to the former brand until the transition is complete. Your Maine Coon will have enough adjustments to make in its new home, so offer new products gradually, and keep increasing the amounts until your cat accepts the change.

CAT CARRIERS

Even if you never show your Maine Coon at a cat show, it is a good idea to purchase a sturdy carrying case. Trips to the veterinarian can be less traumatic if your cat is safe and secure in its carrier. In fact, you will find the carrier to be quite handy *any time* you need to transport or confine your cat. It is never safe for a cat to be allowed to wander around inside an automobile (or any other vehicle) without some type of restraint. Be sure to select a carrier that is well ventilated and one that is large enough for a grown cat to lie down in comfortably. Although a kitten may look lost inside a large carrier, remember that your kitten will one day be a large cat!

Above: Cats are very clean animals, so it is important to keep your Maine Coon's litter box clean at all times; otherwise, it will choose another spot to deposit its wastes.

Children must learn to respect cats. Teach your children to be gentle with their pets and show them how to properly pick up and hold a cat. Jason and Cheryl Bass. Photo: Sharyn Bass.

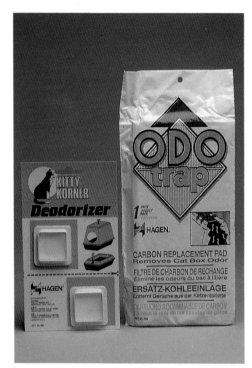

Left: You can purchase special deodorizing units for litter boxes that will virtually eliminate any unpleasant odors. **Below:** Litter boxes come in a wide variety of styles and sizes. Those manufactured today are lightweight and easy to clean. Photos courtesy Rolf C. Hagen Corp.

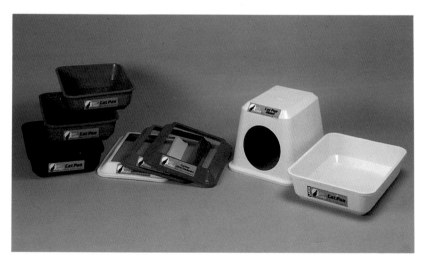

Right: There are a number of safe, effective products available for the treatment of minor conditions. When using any such product, read the label carefully and follow the instructions as noted. Photo courtesy Rolf C. Hagen Corp. **Below:** Maine Coon dam and kittens. Groom your pet on a regular basis to keep it looking its best. Photo: Isabelle Francais.

THE SCRATCHING POST

An instinctive behavior of all domestic felines is the desire to scratch and claw in order to slough off the thin outer nail coverings that are constantly being shed. Scratching is necessary, therefore, to keep a cat's claws in good condition. Unfortunately (for cat owners) felines love to scratch and claw such expensive items as furniture, carpeting, and custom draperies. Before your Maine Coon has a chance to develop such bad habits, it is important to provide it with some type of a scratching post the very first day you bring your new pet home. Place your Maine Coon on the scratching post and while holding its paws firmly in your hands, make scratching motions on the post. If this is repeated often enough, your cat will soon learn what you desire.

There are a variety of scratching posts commercially available. Just be sure that the one you choose for your cat is long enough for it to stretch out on. Many cats especially love the carpet-covered structures that stretch from floor to ceiling, the ones with many levels to rest on and cubby holes to sleep in.

Should your Maine Coon start scratching something other than its designated scratching post, keep a water pistol or spray bottle handy. An occasional squirt of water is a most effective deterrent. Keeping your cat's claws clipped is also important (see the section on Grooming).

FEEDING YOUR MAINE COON

The nutritional needs of cats are rather complex; therefore, it is important to provide your Maine Coon with a well-balanced diet. Proper diet ensures good health and growth, the results of which can be seen in a cat's general appearance. A healthy cat will be active and will have a hearty appetite; its coat will be clean, soft, and lustrous; its eyes will be clear and bright; and its nose and ears will be clean and free of foreign matter. Cats that are fed appropriately will be able to stave off sickness better than cats that are not receiving the proper nutrients.

Felines are carnivorous (meat eaters) and require large amounts of *high quality* protein such as meat, poultry, fish, egg yolks, and (small quantities of) milk. Although protein is certainly an important part of a cat's diet, it should be offered along with the proper amounts of fats, carbohydrates, vitamins, and minerals. Check with the person from whom you purchased your Maine Coon and with your veterinarian to see what the specific requirements are for your cat. When you bring your new pet home, continue feeding it the food to which it is accustomed. If you decide to change your cat's diet, do so *gradually* by adding progressively larger and larger amounts of the new brand of cat food to the old brand until the change has been made.

There are a variety of good commercially prepared cat foods available which provide all of the essentials your cat needs for growth and development. Most of these products are "nutritionally complete" or "nutritionally balanced" and meet the minimum nutritional requirements established by the National Research Council, so it makes sense to feed these products to your Maine Coon. Always read the label of each food product you purchase so that you know what you are buying. Some cat owners prefer to prepare their own meals for their felines; however, it is difficult to know if these cats that are fed homemade preparations are, in fact, getting a well-balanced diet. For this reason, home-cooked meals are not recommended.

Generally, there are three types of cat food available and all three should be included in your cat's diet. There are dry, semi-moist, and canned varieties, and all have their advantages and disadvantages. Dry foods usually

Grooming is an essential part of the regular care of your
Maine Coon. There are a variety of grooming tools
available that can help to keep your favorite feline
looking its very best. Photo courtesy Interplex Labs.

are less expensive than semi-moist and canned foods, and they are convenient, since they can be left out all day for your cat to nibble on whenever the need arises. These dry, hard morsels work well to remove tartar from the cat's teeth and thus help keep the teeth and gums clean and in good condition; however, there is relatively little moisture content in these foods, so *always* supply clean, fresh water alongside your cat's food dishes. Dry foods should not be fed exclusively, especially to cats that are prone to urinary problems such as Feline Urologic Syndrome. FUS affects both male and female cats and is caused by salts in the urine that build up and form bladder stones. Sometimes these stones are passed through the cat's urethra during urination, but sometimes they may plug up and block the urinary tract. When blockage occurs, poisonous wastes cannot be excreted and are forced back into the cat's bloodstream . . . death can result. After a great deal of research, many veterinarians believe that while some dry foods may not actually *cause* FUS, they may aggravate the problem (due to their high ash content). Often, it is recommended that these foods be eliminated from the diet of those cats that suffer from this urinary disorder, in order to help alleviate the problem.

Semi-moist cat food has a higher moisture content than dry foods and is slightly more flavorful. Like dry foods, these semi-moist tidbits contain preservatives which enable them to be left out for periods of time without spoiling (shorter periods than dry food). Dry and semi-moist foods should not be fed exclusively, as they often lack certain vitamins, minerals, and fatty acids that have been lost during processing. Both of these foods should be included in your cat's diet, along with canned, moist foods.

Canned cat foods are usually more expensive than the other two types of cat foods, but they contain more vitamins, minerals, and water. Most cats that are fed moist cat foods do not need much water (although water should *always* be available, even if your cat seldom drinks it). Most cats seem to find canned foods especially palatable, perhaps because these foods are less processed. Be certain to remove any uneaten food, though, since it spoils easily.

As previously mentioned, it is wise to offer combinations of all three varieties of cat foods; all are important in your cat's diet. Offer different foods and flavors so that your Maine Coon does not become a "finicky" eater, but instead, becomes accustomed to several foods.

Pregnant and lactating females have special nutritional requirements. In particular, they need additional calcium and vitamins in their diet (to aid in their own milk production), but always check first with your veterinarian who will know what your queen's specific nutritional needs are. (Note: cat fanciers refer to whole or unaltered females as "queens.") Remember that anything you add to your queen's diet may be passed on to her kittens, so do not experiment with her diet without your veterinarian's supervision.

Young kittens require a special diet when they are weaned from their mother. Most young kittens between the ages of five and eight weeks will begin to accept an occasional substitute for their mother's milk. This substitute food may consist of strained baby food (beef or chicken) mixed with a small amount of evaporated milk. You may have to place the first few mouthfuls of food directly into the kitten's mouth until it gets used to the idea of eating solid food. Once the kitten has begun to eat baby food in this manner, you can gradually mix a little canned (moist) cat food in with the baby food. When the kitten reaches eight to ten weeks of age, you can introduce the dry and semi-moist foods. As always, consult your veterinarian about your kitten's diet.

Although some cats are seldom seen drinking from their water dishes, don't be fooled into thinking that cats do not need water in their diet. Be certain that your Maine Coon *always* has easy access to clean, fresh water. Photo: Sharyn Bass.

Orphaned or rejected kittens require very special care in order to survive their first few weeks of kittenhood. If, for some reason, your queen refuses to nurse her newborn kittens, *you* must intervene and supply the needed nourishment for the newborns immediately, if they are to survive. If you plan to breed a female Maine Coon (or several Maine Coons), be sure to keep plenty of kitten milk replacer (formula) and pet nurser kits (which consist of bottles and nipples) on hand. Purchase these things *before* your queen is about to give birth, so that in the event she refuses to nurse her kittens (or is incapable of nursing), you will be prepared to offer nourishment.

There are a variety of food and water dishes available at most pet shops, and these dishes should be washed every day with hot water and a mild detergent and rinsed well to remove any soap residue.

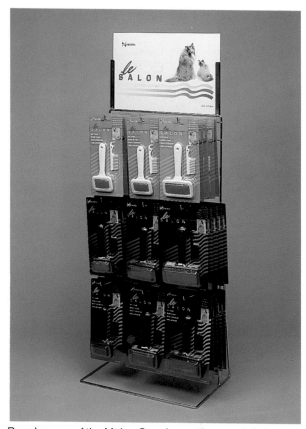

Regular care of the Maine Coon's coat is especially important in order to remove loose dead hairs. Brushes, combs, and other grooming tools are available at your pet shop. Your pet shop dealer can advise you as to which are most suitable for your cat. Photo courtesy of Rolf C. Hagen Corp.

GROOMING AND GOOD HEALTH

Basic grooming of the Maine Coon should begin as early as possible, preferably when it is a few weeks old. A kitten that has become adjusted to being groomed will not pose a problem when it reaches adulthood; therefore, the earlier good grooming procedures are begun, the easier it will be for you to groom your cat. With a young kitten, grooming sessions should last only a few minutes; as the kitten matures, grooming time can be extended according to the cat's patience. If you are planning to show your kitten, it is imperative that the cat be used to being handled and groomed.

Brushing is necessary for the beauty and health of your Maine Coon, and it can begin when the kitten is just a few weeks old. Brushing will remove dead hair, and it will help stimulate the cat's circulation, which, in turn, will promote a healthy coat. If dead hair is not removed periodically, it will interfere with the growth of any new coat. It will also cause hairballs to form, which lodge in the cat's stomach. These hairballs (wads of hair) cause the cat to vomit and cough and they can lead to constipation. As the cat attempts to groom and clean itself, the dead, loose hair is swallowed and forms a tight ball in the stomach or intestines. Although the easiest way to avoid this problem is by regular brushing or combing the cat, there are hairball remedies, available in most pet shops, which will eliminate hairballs (should they occur) by lubricating the cat's digestive tract. Add a small amount (one teaspoon) of mineral or vegetable oil to the cat's food, or place petroleum jelly on the cat's tongue about once a week. These are good home remedies.

All cats, no matter what type of coat they have, should be brushed at least once a week. Longhaired breeds need more attention than shorthaired breeds, such as the Siamese, and the long coat should be brushed a few times a week to keep it in good condition. Maine Coons have a fairly large amount of long hair and undercoat, and at times when they are shedding (such as in the spring of the year), it will become necessary to brush them almost daily.

It is also advisable to acquaint your Maine Coon kitten with having its claws clipped. Although the procedure is not complicated and can be mastered in a few sessions, the person from whom you purchased your Maine Coon should be glad and willing to explain the procedure to you and to clip your kitten's claws before you take it home. If you plan to show your cat, you must have all claws clipped before it is judged. Remember, however, that a *declawed* cat is not allowed to enter any competition.

To clip your kitten's claws, grasp a paw in your left hand with the kitten's body supported between your left arm and your body so it cannot make any sudden movements. Hold the clippers in your right hand. Left-handed people should reverse this procedure; hold the kitten against the right side of your body and clip with your left hand. (Many breeders prefer the regular claw clippers, designed for cats, which can be purchased from a pet shop.) In order to clearly see the claw, you must push back the paw pad from above and beneath the toe so the claw will be fully extended. Once the claw is extended, clip it, being careful not to cut into the "quick," which can easily be seen as a long red vein. On your first attempt to clip your kitten's claws, do not cut too close to the quick. If you accidentally cut the quick, the claw may bleed. Clip only the very tip of the claw until the cat is familiar with the procedure, squirms less, and your confidence is firm. Claws will need to be clipped about once a week, but this will save you from unintentional scratches and will also save the upholstery of your fine furniture.

While you are trimming the claws, it is a good idea to check the cat's paw pads for any cuts or injuries,

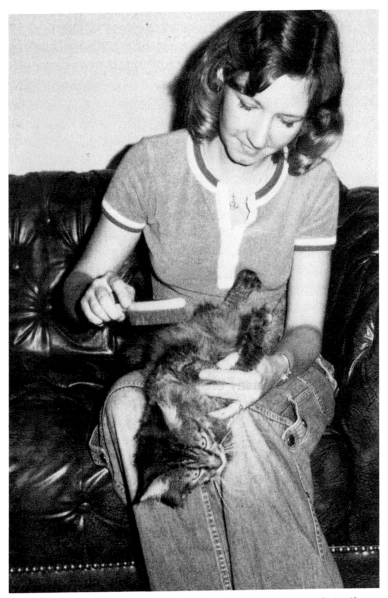

Maine Coons do not need the daily grooming attention that other longhaired breeds need (unless, of course, yours is a show cat); however, regular brushing will help keep the Maine Coon's coat beautifully conditioned. Photo: Ron Reagan.

Show cats should be bathed before each show in order to present them at their very best. Be certain to use a shampoo specially formulated for cats. Photo courtesy Rolf C. Hagen Corp.

especially if your pet is allowed to venture outdoors. A small scratch will probably heal without any assistance, but a larger cut on the pad will take quite a while to heal, since the cat will be constantly stepping on it. This could lead to an infection, which may warrant a visit to your veterinarian.

Although the Maine Coon's ears are very well protected by the tufts of hair surrounding them, they should be checked frequently and cleaned when necessary. A slightly damp cotton ball will suffice for this purpose or possibly a cotton swab, if care is taken not to probe too deeply into the ear. You must never insert anything into the cat's ear any further than you can see. The Maine Coon's ears are quite sensitive and any probing in the ear could cause a great deal of distress and possible injury.

Should you find that your Maine Coon's ears have a dark, crusty material in them, you should consult your veterinarian. This debris is caused by ear mites and the problem should be alleviated as quickly as possible. Your veterinarian will be glad to show you how to clean your cat's ears and will most likely give you medication to take home with you. Your cat's hearing is very important, so do not neglect its ears.

GROOMING FOR SHOW

The Maine Coon Cat, for the purposes of grooming and showing, is considered a longhaired cat. Thus, the grooming techniques used for the Maine Coon are like those used for any other longhaired cat, such as the Persian or Himalayan. The main difference is that the Maine Coon does not require the *constant* grooming which the other longhairs require.

Should the coat of your cat become somewhat oily, it will need a bath before showing. Contrary to what many people believe, cats do not always hate water and can become accustomed to being bathed periodically. Although a very young kitten does not need and should not have a bath, bathing can begin by the time the kitten is about three months old. Make sure the kitten is dried thoroughly after its bath; cats can catch colds. Before you begin to bathe your kitten, however, be sure to clip its claws.

Normal house-cats that do not go outdoors rarely need a bath, although an occasional bath does help keep the coat in good condition. A show cat, however, should be bathed before each show, unless you have a show every weekend, in which case bathing a cat once a week would do harm to the natural oils in the coat. Your cat should be presented at the show in a clean, healthy condition, free of fleas (or other parasites), and beautifully brushed and powdered.

It is probably best to bathe your Maine Coon about a week before the show and to touch the coat up with small additions of grooming powder throughout the week. This is not a hard and fast rule; your cat's coat type must be considered. Some cats have rather dry, dull coats and should not be bathed too often. Other cats have very oily coats and should be bathed frequently in order to look their best. With a little experimentation, you can usually learn when your cat looks its best—bathed a week or more before the show, or bathed two days before the show, and so on.

Your cat or kitten can be bathed in the bathtub or sink, whichever you prefer. It may be best to give the first few baths in the sink, as a large tub of water may frighten a small kitten. Only a few inches of water in the sink is all that is necessary. Running water often scares a cat and can get both of you off on the wrong foot—or paw, as the case may be. Scaring your cat the first time it has a bath will make it twice as unmanageable the next time you try to bathe it. And remember to check the temperature of the water before you put your cat or kitten into it.

You will need pet shampoo (made especially for cats), a brush, a washcloth and a few towels close by so you won't have to leave the wet kitten to gather your equipment. The animal should be brushed very thoroughly *before* bathing. Now you are ready to begin.

Slowly lower the cat or kitten into the water and talk to it reassuringly. A good, steady grip on the cat will help to avoid panic, especially if the cat feels its feet may slip on the smooth surface. As soon as the cat is in the water, take the washcloth and wet the cat all over with clear water, while holding the cat still with one hand. (The washcloth is also used to wipe the cat's face and eyes, which sometimes collect matter in the corners.) Pour a small amount of shampoo from the neck down to the back, and then starting at the neck, begin to wash the cat with your hands or the washcloth, whichever you prefer. It is important to talk softly to your cat during its first bath, thus reassuring it by your voice.

After the cat (or kitten) has been lathered with shampoo, it is very important to rinse every trace of soap out of its coat. Soap residue will dry out the coat, cause dandruff, and give it a harsh, dull appearance. It is important that your cat have a sleek, shiny coat (but not oily), especially if you intend to show your Maine Coon. Rinse the cat at least twice with clear, clean water poured from a pitcher or container; do not rinse with the same bath water. Excess water can then be squeezed gently out of the longhaired areas by using your hands and applying slight pressure.

Once the cat is thoroughly rinsed, it should be wrapped in a towel and gently massaged. As the hair of Maine Coons can hold a large amount of water, the first towel you use will quickly become wet. Now is the time to use another towel to finish the drying. (Incidentally, if you haven't been lucky enough to master claw clipping yet, this would be an appropriate time, since the cat's attention is elsewhere. Do make sure, however, that the animal is kept warm while you clip its claws.)

The best method for thoroughly drying your cat is to use a handheld hair dryer. Many cats are afraid of the noise made by hair dryers, and it may be necessary to towel-dry your cat and place it in a warm spot to dry off completely. If a hair dryer is used, be sure that the dryer is *not* on a high setting and *not* held too close to the coat, as this may cause discomfort or burns. And, as with young humans, the cat should not be allowed outside or in a draft until it is *completely* dry.

After the cat is totally dry, you can brush and comb the coat in order to fluff it up around the tail, britches, stomach, and ruff. It should be noted that if the animal is not completely dry when you begin brushing, you may pull out new hair growth, which could severely damage a show coat.

One problem that may be encountered with adult males of all breeds of cat is "stud tail," the name given to the oily hair at the base of the cat's back and tail. It makes the coat look oily and should be alleviated before your male is presented in a cat show. Do not brush the base of the cat's tail vigorously, as this will stimulate the glands and add to the problem. Wash the affected area with a mild liquid detergent (such as those made for washing dishes), as this will cut through the oil. This detergent should not be used on the entire coat, but *only* on the stud tail area. After the area is washed, you can proceed to wash the rest of the cat with your usual cat shampoo.

If your cat is allowed outside, there may be times when its coat becomes matted. These mats could form any place where the hair is long, such as the ruff, tail,

Regular grooming is a necessary part of Maine Coon care and it probably helped this handsome brown tabby-and-white male, Sup. Gr. Ch. Friscoon's Buffalo Bill, achieve his polished look. Breeders/owners: Pat Herrmann and Robert Salerno. Photo: Robert Pearcy.

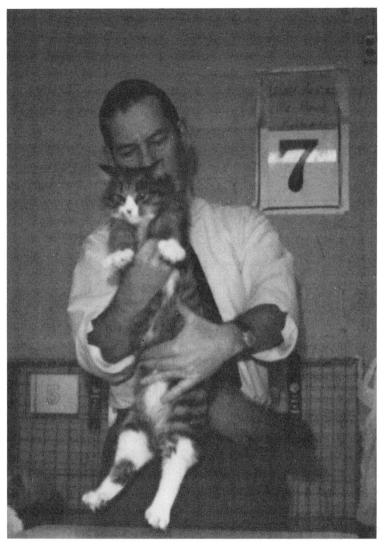

In addition to bathing a show cat and clipping its claws, make sure that it is in excellent condition. It should be free of both external and internal parasites, and it should have a healthy glow. CFA judge Walter Friend checks Ch. Patchet's Samantha of Schick for weight, conformation, and balance. Photo: Sharyn Bass.

stomach, sides, or britches. Mats must be removed carefully, both to prevent injury to the cat and to save as much of the coat as possible. Once a cat's coat becomes badly matted, it often takes quite a few months for it to be restored to the proper condition for showing. This is why it is important to groom your Maine Coon regularly, so as to prevent these unsightly mats from becoming a problem.

Pet shops stock a variety of combs, brushes, and grooming tools, including special combs for the removal of mats. Another good tool for removing mats is a seam ripper, which can be purchased from any sewing center. This is a sharp-pointed instrument, and great care must be taken while using it. If the cat's hair is matted close to the skin, it may take hours to properly remove the mat. The seam ripper should be moved very slowly between the mat and the skin, while at the same time trying to save as much of the coat as possible. Because this is a time-consuming procedure, it may be necessary for you to work at it off-and-on for the next few days. It is certainly better to brush the cat regularly to avoid all of this, than to try both your nerves, and your cat's, to their limits—as well as to risk the possibility of injuring your cat, should it make any sudden movements.

Many exhibitors use grooming powder to make their cat's coat look full and fluffy. With the Maine Coon, however, only the parts of the coat that have long hair should be so treated. A baby powder or pure talcum powder can be used equally well. For the male Maine Coon with a stud tail problem, a good powder to use on this area would be NP-27, which can be purchased wherever human foot care products are sold. This powder is germicidal but must not be used on young kittens.

Black cats should *never*, under any circumstances, be powdered, as a black Maine Coon depends upon a shiny coat to look its best and any powder products will dry out

Wetting and reassuring Ch. Sergeant Whiskers of Schick during bath time is author Sharyn Bass. **Opposite:** Be sure to wet the cat's entire coat, and then apply shampoo made especially for cats. Photos: Ron Reagan.

Classic brown tabby Maine Coon owned by Judy Friedman. Photo: Isabelle Francais.

the coat. Black-and-white Maine Coons pose a problem. Although it is all right to powder the white portions of the cat, it is extremely tedious to avoid getting the powder on the black portions. The solution then is to avoid powdering bi-colors altogether.

The Maine Coon will be shown to advantage if you powder only the longhaired parts and don't dry out or disturb the rest of the coat (such as the back) which should remain sleek and shiny.

After brushing the powder completely out of the longhaired portions of the coat of a tabby, use the comb on the sides and back to make the markings as distinct as possible.

Remember that every trace of powder must be removed before you put a cat in the judging ring. Should a judge place your cat on the judging table and a puff of powder rise into the air, the cat could be disqualified, and you certainly will be embarrassed. Powder can be used effectively to make the Maine Coon look its best—but any powder used to change the true color or appearance of the cat is a serious offense and will cause much disruption in your relations with the judge and the other exhibitors. Judges are fully aware of all the "tricks" exhibitors sometimes use to alter the appearance of their cats, and although the judge may choose not to publicly embarrass you, your cat may not be put up for the wins it may have deserved had it been presented honestly.

Remember also that a cat must be in superior condition when it is shown. Although grooming sets off the strong points of a healthy cat, it doesn't cover up the weak points of an unhealthy one. The cat must maintain a good weight through proper diet and be without any evidence of worms or external parasites. Any cat having ear mites, fleas, or ticks poses a problem to other exhibitors and their cats, for these parasites can be picked up at shows and carried home to what had been a parasite-free environment. Also, judges do not take kindly to handling cats that are flea-infested and obviously not properly taken care of.

The Maine Coon is a beautiful feline and should be presented in the best possible manner. It should have a clean, lustrous coat and clean ears, eyes, and nose that are free of foreign matter; it should be healthy and of good weight; it should be impeccably groomed and free of parasites. When your Maine Coon is in excellent condition, even when it may not make a big win at the show, you can still be justifiably proud of owning a beautiful and healthy cat. It is a very good feeling you get when a spectator comments on the beauty of your cat, or the judge remarks on how well-presented it is.

Rinse your Maine Coon thoroughly; otherwise, whatever traces of shampoo are left will dull the coat and dry it out. Use only clean, clear water for rinsing. Photo: Ron Reagan.

Opposite:
Be sure to wrap your Maine Coon in a large absorbent towel and gently massage the cat to blot up excess water. Allow your cat to dry off in a *warm* area so that it does not become chilled and catch a cold. A hand-held hair dryer also can be used to finish drying the cat's coat. Photo: Ron Reagan.

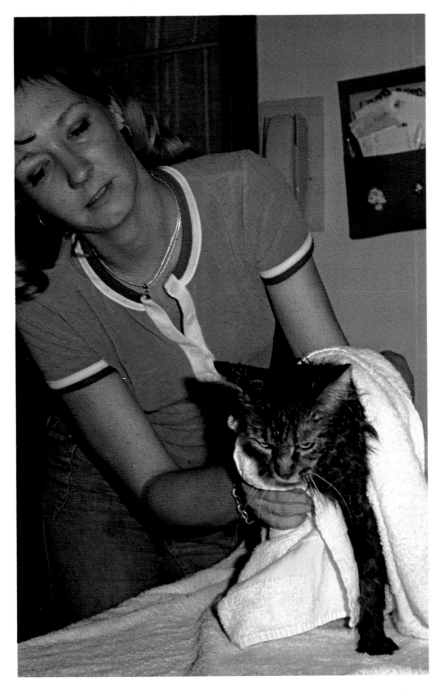

Breeding and Delivery

The decision as to whether or not you should breed your Maine Coon is yours alone. Everyone loves furry little kittens and they are a joy to have around but not *everyone* wants them around. It is a tremendous responsibility to insure that all of the kittens you may allow to be born will find good homes; it is wise to have homes already lined up *before* you breed your cat. It would be unwise and unjust to bring kittens into the world and then take them to a shelter to be put to sleep. This is not a cheerful thought, but it is one which must be considered. Most people do not realize that there are thousands of darling kittens and puppies put to sleep every year, either because an owner was negligent and allowed the pet to run loose and breed free, or "thought" they wanted the babies but had made no provision for finding homes for them.

If, by chance, you believe there is a ready market for kittens and that you will make some easy money—put the thought immediately out of your head. The cost of raising kittens is amazingly high when you consider shots, litter material and a wholesome diet, and these are merely the basics. Should your queen have trouble delivering, you may need to call your veterinarian—and right away you are building a deficit. Even breeders with show quality kittens sometimes have difficulty finding good homes for them; the prices received for the kittens may

Maine Coon queens are excellent mothers and are quite capable of caring for their young. Let nature take its course, and lend a hand only when necessary, especially if a kitten is having difficulty nursing. Photo: Sharyn Bass.

not even make up for the expense of raising and showing their parents.

Many others who want to breed their pet cats believe it is good experience for their children to watch. Although the breeding and birth of animals is a wonderful thing to observe, it would be best not to bring unwanted animals into an overcrowded world. The children may get an education on the birth process, but having to give away beloved kittens to a shelter would outweigh any good things they may have learned—including compassion for animals.

If, after thinking about and accepting this responsibility you still want to breed your Maine Coon, we wish you success. Let's assume you have an unaltered female Maine Coon—one that meets the Standard and is in the

Most reputable breeders recommend that pet-quality kittens be altered (when they reach sexual maturity) if they are not to be bred. If you *are* interested in breeding your Maine Coon, be certain that homes will be found for all of the kittens. This litter of six-week old Schick kittens was well planned. Breeders: Sharyn and Richard Bass. Photo: Ron Reagan.

Opposite:
Ch. Schick's Razor Sharp, a black kitten pictured at six weeks of age. Breeders: Sharyn and Richard Bass. Photo: Ron Reagan.

Male cats, particularly those that have not been neutered, will instinctively spray urine on a variety of objects in an effort to "mark" their territory. This behavior is perfectly normal, although it can be rather unpleasant for their owners. Stud pants will help to control this spraying problem. Photo: Ron Reagan.

Cats that are allowed to roam freely outdoors will breed indiscriminately, and, thus, great numbers of stray kittens will result. The breeding of cats should be well planned and supervised indoors where, hopefully, conditions will be more favorable. Photo: Ron Reagan.

peak of health. The health of your female is very important. She should be fed a good diet, be free of any
parasites or illness, and should have her vaccinations up-
to-date. If these things have not been taken care of *before*
your queen is bred, you may encounter some problems;
infections, for example, can easily be transmitted from
the queen to her kittens.

Your queen should be bred to the best possible male
Maine Coon you can find, even if it means traveling to a
cattery some distance away. The purpose of breeding
Maine Coons should be to better the breed so that your
cat's offspring will be even better than it is. This is not
possible if just any stud (an unaltered male) is chosen.
The stud should also be the picture of good health and
should have good Maine Coon characteristics. For example, if your queen does not have good ear tufts, you
should try to find a stud who has *extra good* ear tufts, as
you want to breed this characteristic into your new line.

"Two faults do not make a right." Should your queen
have an extra long, but very slender body, do not breed
her to a male with a short, cobby body, as *neither* of these
types is good. The kittens will have bodies either like
that of your queen or that of the stud. In this respect,
nature does not compromise; the kittens will not have the
nice, medium-to-long, hefty body required in the Standard. In general, they will take after either one of the
parents and not take on those characteristics that lie
somewhere between the two extremes. So do not try to
compensate for one fault by introducing another.

Once a stud has been chosen and your queen comes into season, she will call in a non-characteristic loud,
raucous voice, yet be much more affectionate. Now the
breeding itself can take place. The female will call almost
constantly, making life at home nearly unbearable for
you. But it is best not to breed a queen at the time of her
very first calling episode; she needs a chance to mature

Play is an important part of a kitten's growth and development. Check your local pet shop for a complete line of safe toys for your Maine Coon. Photo: Ron Reagan.

Littermates Schick's Kabuki and Ch. Schick's Shendorah Valentine huddle together for warmth and companionship. Breeders: Sharyn and Richard Bass. Owner (Kabuki): Melanie Robertson. Owner (Shendorah): Sharyn and Richard Bass. Photo: Ron Reagan.

This carpet-covered structure serves a dual purpose: as a cat chalet, it is a suitable "house" for your Maine Coon to relax in; as a scratching post, it is a useful piece of equipment for helping your cat keep its claws in good condition. Photo: Ron Reagan.

113

properly and should be bred either during her second season or after she is one year old. This allows her to grow physically (so her body can cope with carrying and delivering kittens) and grow emotionally (so as to accept the responsibility of caring properly for the kittens).

The first time your queen is bred, it is better to breed her to a stud who is experienced. Likewise, the first time a male is bred, it is best to breed him to a queen who has previously had kittens. For the most part, all studs usually perform better when they remain at home and the queen is brought to the stud's quarters; this is the way most breeding is accomplished. Should you have to send your queen away to another cattery, be sure to obtain verification that the cattery and its studs are clean and disease-free. The owner of the stud, in return, will require a health certificate from your veterinarian verifying the good health of your queen. These are precautions that should be maintained, for both your queen and the stud.

When the queen and the stud are first introduced, there may be quite a bit of spitting and apparent dislike for each other. Given time, however, things will usually work out and you can return your queen to her home and look forward to kittens. Should either cat reject the idea of breeding, it usually means that the queen is not in the proper stage of estrus (which is usually a few days from the time she begins calling), and the stud instinctively knows this. When the time is right and the two cats are introduced, the male will not give up and will continue to court the queen until he is successful. There are few things that will cause a Maine Coon stud to become discouraged; if he *does* become discouraged, however, do not become upset. Wait until the next day and try again. When the time is right, both cats know it and proceed without coaching from anyone. The noises produced at this time can be quite disturbing to a new breeder's innocent ears, but it is all part of the process. Things may get a little rough, but as long as both cats are not harmed, they should be allowed to continue uninterrupted.

After a short period of hissing and apparent mutual dislike, the male will approach the female. Timing plays an important part here. A stud will sometimes wait for hours while trying to approach the female from the correct position, but he will rarely become discouraged. At the proper time, the stud will jump toward the queen and grasp her by the neck while sliding his body on top of hers. If the position is not correct, he will try to adjust it. If he cannot assume the correct position, he will back off and try again.

Once the neck of the female is firmly in the jaws of the male, she will crouch lower and raise her abdomen while moving her tail to the side. The male will push against her until what he feels is the proper time—and for the supervising breeder, this can seem to last an eternity. It is very important, however, that breeding animals *never* be left alone, and no matter how long it takes, you should be there with them, supervising. Some people might feel that this is an insult to nature's experienced way of doing things, but there are often times, such as during an animal's labor, when even nature can use a helping hand.

When the time is right, the stud will insert his penis into the queen and continue to hold onto her neck until the breeding is accomplished, at which time the queen will scream as if she were dying. Do not be alarmed by this. The scream, which will last only a few seconds, is a natural part of feline breeding and will tell you that the male has been successful. The female will strike out at the male as soon as he releases her neck, and it is important for him to be able to make a hasty retreat. After he has retreated, the queen will begin to lick herself and calm down, allowing the stud to clean himself also, and keep a wary eye on the queen.

115

Shy Precious of Schick, a brown mackerel patched tabby—one of the first patched tabbies shown when they were accepted by CFA for championship status. Breeder: Arlene Rodgers. Owners: Sharyn and Richard Bass. Photo: Ron Reagan.

This young six-week old red mackerel tabby kitten, Schick's General MacArthur is still too young to leave his mother and littermates. Sire: Ch. Sergeant Whiskers of Schick. Dam: Shy Precious of Schick. Breeders/owners: Sharyn and Richard Bass. Photo: Sharyn Bass.

Many times breeders will breed the cats again the next day to make sure that the queen is impregnated. The second breeding usually will take half the time and the two will seem to get along better. It is relatively hard to estimate how long any breeding will take, as cats' temperaments differ somewhat. Some may take hours just to "size each other up" before getting down to the business of copulation.

Now that you know your queen has been successfully bred, you must wait, usually between 60 and 65 days, for the arrival of the kittens. The queen will not seem to change immediately. Her nipples will take on a rather pinkish color, which can be noted about two weeks later, and this will be the first true sign of pregnancy. Eventually, you will notice that her appetite increases and she will begin to put on extra weight. At this time, it is doubly important to feed her a good, healthy diet to ensure a safe delivery and the birth of healthy kittens.

Once your female begins to eat incessantly and starts putting on extra weight, the birth of kittens soon will follow. Give her a good diet rich in vitamins and especially rich in calcium, which she is using up to form the bones of her kittens. Should the unborn kittens be deprived of essential nutrients, it will be very hard for them to grow properly after birth and you may have some serious problems on your hands.

Before your queen's kittens are due, acquaint her with a queening box (also called a maternity or kittening box). This will be the place where it is hoped she will give birth to and house her kittens until they are old enough to take off on their own. The appearance of the box is of little importance, but it should meet certain requirements:

1. It should be long enough for the queen to stretch out in while giving birth and nursing the new kittens.
2. It should be free from drafts.
3. It should be raised off the ground a few inches for proper ventilation.
4. It should be shielded from strong light.
5. It should be sturdily built but with a *soft* interior.

These requirements are necessary for the safety and comfort of your queen and the newborns.

The easiest and most convenient type of box to use is a clean, strong cardboard box. It should have a small opening cut out of one side, but not cut all the way down to the floor. In this way, the queen can get in and out easily but the kittens will not fall out accidentally or climb out and wander around before their mother wants them to. You can also cut the top portion of the box on three sides to allow you to lift the lid and look in on the family.

When you purchase a Maine Coon, regardless of the source, choose one that is obviously active, alert, and the picture of good health. The coat should be lustrous and soft to the touch. The eyes should be clear and bright. The nose should be clear and free of any discharge. Check the ears to see that they are clean and free of foreign matter. Photo: Ron Reagan.

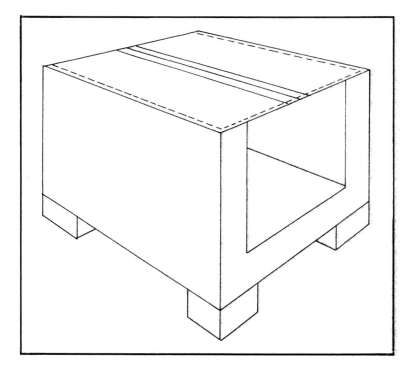

QUEENING BOX

Cut out and remove the center portion of one side of a large, sturdy cardboard box so that the queen will be able to exit and enter the box whenever necessary. The top flaps should be taped closed with masking tape or packing tape, and then three sides of the top should be cut (along the dotted lines) so that the top can be easily lifted to check on the family occasionally. Keep the lid down at all times. Place the queening box a small distance off the floor on something solid for support, such as four uniformly cut wood blocks. Illustration: Carol A. Kyle.

The box should be covered with clean material on the inside so the kittens will be warm and comfortable. Towels are not very suitable until the kittens are somewhat older, as they may snag their tiny claws in the material and not be able to move to their mother to nurse. Clean sheets are good, as they will not catch the claws and the kittens can be easily observed against them.

Unless the queen is given ample time to become used to the box, she may decide to have her kittens elsewhere— somewhere dangerous or, at the very least, unclean, and kittens ought to be born in a sanitary environment. It is important that you be able to get to the queen when she delivers in case she needs your assistance. Well in advance of the delivery, acquaint her with the box so that she will feel it is her very own.

If you have allowed your queen to go outdoors, there is an added danger that she may go off and not be able to make it home before labor begins. In her urgency to get home to safety (while strange things are happening to her), she may give birth to the kittens at different stops along the way. Also, should she have the kittens outdoors and a placenta (birth sac covering the kitten) or dead kitten remained in her uterus, infection would begin and by the time she finally arrived home she would be in very bad shape. So, do not allow your queen outside *at all* during the last week of her pregnancy.

As the time draws close for her delivery, she may become somewhat nervous. Give her an added amount of affection and companionship. She will probably show the signs of impending birth, such as crying softly, following you everywhere, refusing to eat, or "testing out" the nesting box. Many times, however, queens will act perfectly normal before delivery and not give a clue as to when the expected event will take place. When the arrival time is within one week, cancel any vacations or other plans that may keep you away from home. Your queen may need your help with her first litter, and it is best to remain with her as much as possible. Even if you are not required to assist in the delivery, your presence at this important time in her life is some compensation for the joy she has given you.

It is very important to have a number of items ready in case you should need them during her delivery. All of

Above: Ch. Schick's Macooca L'Noir, a black female kitten pictured at six weeks of age. Breeders: Sharyn and Richard Bass. Owner: Debbi Burke. **Opposite above:** Cats are creatures of comfort, and cat sofabeds are the answer for even the most particular of felines. **Opposite below:** Ch. Schick's Beautiful Dreamer, a brown classic patched tabby female, inspects this colorful scratching post that serves as a resting place for a vigilant kitten! Photos: Ron Reagan.

125

these should be sterilized and kept as clean as possible. You will need a pair of scissors, thread, clean towels and washcloths, and a hot water bottle. Keep all of this equipment together so that it will be ready at hand as your queen begins labor.

At the onset of labor, the queen will become restless and perhaps pant. If she has become used to her box, she will lay down and rest between contractions. Sometimes she may cry. Labor can last for as long as an hour, but do not become alarmed if it continues a little longer; talking to her will help to calm both of you. As long as the contractions are steady and she does not seem to be in great pain, it is best to let nature take its course.

The first kitten will emerge wrapped in its amniotic sac (a fluid-filled sac). The queen will instinctively tear off the portion of the sac covering the kitten's mouth to allow it to breathe. She will remove the rest of the sac, cut the umbilical cord with her teeth and proceed to eat the sac and placenta. You may gasp at this sight, but be assured that it is the most natural thing for the queen to do; the afterbirth provides her with added nutrients. If she had delivered her kittens in the wild, she would have eaten the afterbirth to keep predators from tracing the scent back to the nest. Also, the afterbirth would be the only food she would get until the kittens were old enough to be left alone safely in the nest. Nature has provided this as a natural means of nutrition and protection for the new mother and kittens.

As each kitten is born, the queen will stimulate the kitten's circulation by licking its body. Breathing will be stimulated as the queen licks the remnants of the amniotic sac off the kitten's face (particularly around the nose and mouth). After the kitten is completely cleaned off, the queen will proceed with more contractions and the delivery of another kitten. The first kitten may cry a bit but it will calm down after it starts nursing. After contractions resume, you may take the first kitten and dry it off with a soft washcloth and put it near the warm hot water bottle. Be sure that the hot water bottle is not too hot, as it would burn the kitten's tender skin. It is important at this point to keep the newborns warm until the queen has completed delivery and can attend to them herself. After all the kittens are born, the queen will settle down to nurse them and you can fix yourself a stiff drink!

There are a few things that may force you to lend a helping hand. After delivery of one kitten, the queen may have contractions for an extended period of time but a kitten will not be produced or be only partially visible. Great care must be taken for the sake of both the queen and the kitten. Your hands must be absolutely clean and once again you will need a clean washcloth. You must firmly, but gently, grasp the partially delivered kitten with the washcloth around it to secure your hold. Should the kitten appear dry, you should apply a little mineral oil or petroleum jelly to its coat, push it partway back into the birth canal and wait for the next contraction. When the queen has a hard contraction, you must continue to hold onto the kitten, but DO NOT PULL. The kitten should begin to slide out gradually.

Other problems may be that the kitten is extra large or will be in a breech position (feet first). You may need the help of your veterinarian, who, in extreme cases, may have to perform a Caesarian section. This, however, is very rare in Maine Coons and most often happens with small oriental-type cats.

Many times a young queen with her first litter will become too tired to properly clean a newborn kitten. In this case, *you* must take over. The first thing to do is to pull away the sac from the kitten's face and wipe off all fluids from the nose and mouth so that the kitten may begin breathing. Then, after squeezing the umbilical

cord between your thumb and forefinger for a few seconds, cut the umbilical cord with the sterilized scissors about one inch from the kitten's body. The umbilical cord will probably not produce any blood, but if it does, you can tie the cord off with some sterilized thread. Make a constant check of the umbilical cord for the next few days to be sure that it has not become infected. If this happens, you should notify your veterinarian, who can recommend and prescribe an antiseptic.

If, after you have wiped off all fluids around the kitten's nose and mouth, the kitten still fails to breathe, hold the kitten firmly in one hand with its head against your fingers and its tail resting on your wrist. Next, raise your arm above your head, and keeping your arm unbended, lower your arm in an arc to your side in one swift—but not violently swift—movement. This method gets out any fluids remaining in the kitten's nose and mouth and clears the passages for breathing. If you swing the kitten too fast, its delicate lungs could be injured. It is important to get a new kitten breathing as quickly as possible, and great attention should be paid to this if the kitten has not begun breathing within two minutes. (Although it is better to wait for your veterinarian at a time like this, you may have to step in, in order to save a kitten's life.) After proper breathing is induced, take a washcloth and thoroughly wipe the kitten dry; this further stimulates breathing and circulation and helps to keep the kitten from becoming chilled. Then place the newborn near the warm hot water bottle to wait for nursing time.

Opposite:
Kayenta's Terracotta, a red tabby-and-white male. Sire: Roselu Blue Star. Dam: Kerry-Kits Adamina of Kayenta. Breeder: Alison L. Grinder. Photo: Ron Reagan. If you own a female Maine Coon and you plan to breed her, find the best possible stud you can, one that is healthy and that has good Maine Coon characteristics.

You may think that all of these instructions are complicated and that you could not possibly handle these situations, but should you find it necessary to do any of these things in order to save your queen's life or a kitten's life, you will find yourself doing them automatically without giving it a second thought. Although the delivery of kittens is always a bit trying on human nerves, try to relax and enjoy witnessing the miracle of birth.

The kittens should begin to nurse soon after the mother delivers the last kitten. They may begin crying at this time. Once they begin nursing, you can be sure that all is well. If the queen refuses to nurse the kittens or if they do not seem to be getting any milk (you will know this if they suck and suck but continue to cry), you must use the kitten milk replacer which you had the foresight to get from your veterinarian or pet shop. You will have to hand-feed the kittens until the veterinarian diagnoses the problem.

Check to see that your queen has expelled one placenta for each kitten born. If she has not passed all of the afterbirths, she may, after about three days, become very irritable and refuse to eat. She should be taken to your veterinarian, along with the kittens, to be diagnosed and given treatment.

Kittens are easiest to sex immediately after they are born, while they are still wet. The female genitalia will look like a small "i" and that of the male like a ":" (colon). If there is only one kitten in the litter, it may be hard to decide its sex. By comparing the entire litter, you will soon be able to differentiate the sex of each kitten. If you wait too long to sex the kittens, you will find it more difficult than it would have been when they were first born.

Usually a kitten's eyes will open after about 10 days, but it will take a few days more for the kitten to be able to focus on an object. Once the eyes can focus on you and the kittens begin toddling around, the joy—both of being a kitten and owning one—really begins.

Should you have any questions or believe there is any problem with your queen or her new litter, it is best to get professional advice. Most veterinarians will be pleased to help you, even with a slight problem. Do remember, however, that it is best to contact your veterinarian during his or her working hours, if at all possible. If a problem begins to arise in the early afternoon, do not wait until that night to decide to contact your veterinarian unless a real emergency that could not have been foreseen during the day arises.

Now that your new litter of Maine Coons has arrived and the excitement is over, make two resolutions for their well-being: first, that you will keep them healthy and provide for their safety and happiness; second, that you will allow them to go only to homes that will do the same. After all, it was with your sanction that the kittens came into being and they will be your responsibility until they begin a new life with someone else, who, it is hoped, will love them as much as you do.

Health Care

When you purchase your Maine Coon, be sure to ask for any papers that document the cat or kitten's background. Such information would include a pedigree, registration papers, and medical records (which should include a history of vaccinations, booster shots, and any health problems that may have occurred). Make an appointment to see your veterinarian as soon as you bring your new pet home. Most cats that have been purchased from a breeder should already have had their shots (and there should be written proof of this); if, for some reason, your Maine Coon has not been inoculated against some of the major cat diseases, advise your veterinarian immediately.

Included in this health care chapter are a few of the ailments and diseases that affect cats. The list of problems is in no way complete; however, if you want further information on your cat's health and care, check your local pet shop for copies of these fine books which are published by T.F.H. Publications, Inc., Neptune, New Jersey: *Cat Care* (Thies), *Cat Diseases* (Soderberg), *Cat Owner's Encyclopedia of Veterinary Medicine* (Joshua), and *Illustrated Textbook of Cat Diseases* (The TV Vet).

In most instances, you can prevent the spread of disease simply by making daily observations of your Maine Coon. If your pet seems less active than usual, refuses to eat for more than 48 hours, has diarrhea,

Keep your Maine Coon indoors. Cats that are left outside, unsupervised, are exposed to many dangers that threaten their health and safety: they can get into fights with other cats or other animals; they can be hit by cars; they can contract diseases; they can get lost or stolen; and their beautiful, flowing coats can become tangled and soiled. Photo: Ron Reagan.

vomiting, or strains to urinate, call your veterinarian at once. A cat's coat is usually a sign of its health; normally the fur of a healthy cat should be soft, smooth, and lustrous. If the fur is dull, matted, and not in good condition, this may be a sign that the cat is not feeling well and is neglecting its grooming habits. Do not attempt to treat your cat yourself—*always* seek your veterinarian's advice.

EXTERNAL PARASITES

Most cats are plagued at one time or another with external parasites, including fleas, ticks, and mites. These annoying pests can cause great discomfort to your Maine Coon, not to mention skin diseases, infection, a poor coat, and loss of condition. It is important to check your cat regularly for the presence of these parasites and to eradicate them immediately from the cat and its environment.

Vitamin/mineral and other food supplements can be formulated for general nutritional value or for particular purposes, such as skin and coat enhancement and/or flea and tick elimination. Photo courtesy of Four Paws.

Fleas—Fleas are small, hard-shelled, dark insects that can be found anywhere on the cat's body, especially on the warmest parts. Cats that are flea infested become restless, and may lose weight; their coats may become mildly to severely damaged as a result of the cat's constant scratching and biting. Some cats even become allergic to flea bites and suffer inflammation of the skin.

Female fleas deposit their eggs in such places as sand and dirt, in carpeting, on furniture, or in the cracks and crevices of the floors and walls of your home or cattery. The eggs go through their various stages of development until they finally emerge as young adults. It is the adults that spend their lives on the cat, feeding on the cat's blood. Fleas are also carriers (intermediate hosts) of tapeworms and other diseases.

Flea infestation is difficult to eradicate, as eggs are hatching all the time. Not only must the cat be sprayed and powdered with products specifically designed for the removal of fleas, but the cat's environment also must be disinfected, i.e., wherever the cat eats, sleeps, and plays. There are a number of products, including flea collars, flea sprays, and flea powders, available at most pet shops. Be sure to air all flea collars for 24 hours before placing them on your Maine Coon. Some insecticides are safe to use on cats; however *always check the label* to be certain. Check with your veterinarian if you are in doubt.

Ear Mites—If your Maine Coon constantly scratches or twitches its ears, you may suspect the presence of ear mites. These microscopic parasites live in the cat's ear canals and appear as brown granular matter. Treatment from your veterinarian usually will involve a thorough cleansing of the ears, and a medication will be prescribed. It is important to regularly check your cat's ears to prevent an infestation of these annoying pests. Incidentally, should ear mites line the cat's inner ear canals, deafness could result.

Ticks—There are several different species of ticks—brown ticks and wood ticks, to name a few—but if your cat is not allowed outdoors, the chances of it ever having ticks are small. A tick burrows its head into the flesh of its host, in this case your cat, and fills itself with the cat's blood. Ticks produce infections (some of a particularly dangerous kind) in both humans and other animals and should be removed as soon as possible.

Exercise great care when removing a tick. One method of removal is to firmly grasp the tick with a pair of blunt-end tweezers or forceps and pull it out steadily, being *absolutely certain* that the head is removed with the body. Do not simply yank the tick out, as the head may remain behind, still embedded in the cat's skin, and infection may ensue. Another solution to the problem of tick removal is to douse the tick with a cotton swab that has been soaked in alcohol, vinegar, or acetone (nail polish remover). This will loosen the tick from under the cat's skin; then the tick can be safely and easily removed.

INTERNAL PARASITES

There are a number of different internal parasites that can infect your Maine Coon, but worms—especially roundworms and tapeworms—are the most harmful, particularly to young kittens. Worm infestation often robs a kitten's body of important nutrients and causes the kitten to weaken until it loses its resistance to disease; therefore, early detection is important to prevent further damage .

Veterinarians usually will want a specimen of the cat's stool in order to analyze what type of worms are present. Then, he or she will be able to prescribe the proper treatment. Do not attempt to treat the cat yourself; always seek the advice of your veterinarian.

Roundworms—Roundworms are the worms most frequently found in cats. These parasites are long and thin

It is important for young kittens to be inoculated against the major cat diseases such as Panleukopenia and Feline Viral Rhinotracheitis. These vaccinations, which should be administered by your veterinarian as soon as you bring your new kitten home, are, in most cases, the best means of disease prevention. Photo: Ron Reagan.

Cats that are going to be shown in cat shows should be free of parasites and disease. At "vetted" shows, all entries are first examined by a veterinarian before being allowed to enter the show hall. Photo: Ron Reagan.

in appearance and live in the cat's intestines (sometimes in the stomach). Roundworms vary in size and shape; however their life cycles are essentially the same: roundworm eggs are passed in the cat's feces; cats that come in contact with their own infected feces or with infected soil become re-infected, as the eggs are transmitted to the cat's mouth; the roundworms travel to the cat's intestines where they grow to maturity; the adult roundworms deposit eggs which are again passed in the cat's stool, and the cycle repeats itself. (Note: Cats who are free of parasites also can become afflicted if they, too, come in contact with the infected cat's feces or infected soil.) Besides being passed in the cat's stool, roundworms also can be vomited up. Sanitation is an important means in controlling the spread of roundworms.

Tapeworms—Like roundworms, tapeworms are also found in the cat's intestines. The head of the tapeworm attaches itself to the lining of the cat's intestines, while its body segments (which contain eggs) separate and are passed in the cat's stool. These segments are approximately ¼" long and cream-colored; when dry, they resemble grains of uncooked rice and are darker in color. The tapeworm segments can be seen not only in the cat's feces, but in the fur around the cat's anus. The egg-filled segments passed in the cat's stool are eaten by flea larvae, and as the cat grooms itself (and in so doing ingests the fleas), the tapeworm eggs find their way into the cat's intestines where they mature as adults. The cycle continues as tapeworm body segments are passed through the cat's stool. (Note: This is one good reason why it is important to keep fleas under control, as they are carriers of these contagious parasites.) Infected rodents also can transmit tapeworms to cats that are allowed to roam and hunt outdoors.

Sup. Gr. Ch. Heidi-Ho's Lady Arwen of Mary B. Breeder: Mary M. Condit. Owner: Mary C. Buckmaster. Photo: Courtesy of Mary C. Buckmaster.

Regular health examinations by your veterinarian are a necessary part of Maine Coon care. Early detection of health problems and prompt medical attention are important. Photo: Sharyn Bass.

SOME MAJOR CAT DISEASES

The importance of having your Maine Coon kitten vaccinated against most of the major cat diseases cannot be overemphasized. In most cases, inoculations are the best means of prevention, especially for viral diseases which can wipe out an entire cattery in a short time if not recognized promptly.

Kittens begin to lose their immunity to disease when they stop nursing; therefore, it is necessary to consult with your veterinarian about your kitten's vaccination program. Although it is possible for some viruses and bacteria to affect a cat that *has* been vaccinated, the chances are greater that the cat will overcome the disease, whereas a cat that *has not* been vaccinated will most assuredly succumb to the disease and die shortly thereafter.

Remember that some viruses can remain alive in your household or cattery for weeks or months—even if the infected cat has died. Avoid bringing home a new cat at this time, especially if it has not been properly inoculated; otherwise, your new pet will contract the same virus that killed your first cat. Without fail, check with your veterinarian to find out when you can safely introduce a new cat into your home.

Panleukopenia—Also known as feline infectious enteritis or feline distemper, panleukopenia is a highly contagious viral disease with a high mortality rate, especially among young kittens (although cats of all ages can be afflicted). It is perhaps the most dreaded of all the cat diseases, as it is not easy to detect in its early stages and it progresses quickly. Your Maine Coon could die within 48 hours. Many infected cats show no visible signs of the disease.

Symptoms vary in severity and include loss of appetite, fever, lethargy, depression, vomiting (which can turn yellowish or greenish), diarrhea, and dehydration. In some cases, a cat may sit crouched in front of its water dish, head hanging low, and not be able to drink. As the disease progresses, the cat becomes thin, emaciated, and its coat becomes dull and lusterless.

Since panleukopenia is a difficult disease to treat, the best method of prevention is through vaccinations and booster shots, which are highly effective.

Feline Viral Rhinotracheitis (FVR)—Of all the infectious respiratory diseases that affect cats, FVR is the most severe and widespread. It is caused by a herpes virus, and mortality is high among kittens. Signs of the disease include moderate fever, loss of appetite, depression, salivation, mouth breathing, sneezing, coughing, and watery discharges (which later become purulent) from the eyes and nose. As with panleukopenia, prevention, in the form of inoculations, is the best cure.

Pneumonitis—This is an extremely contagious respiratory disease, especially among young kittens; however, usually it is not fatal. It is caused by the organism *Chlamydia psittaci*, and the symptoms are similar to FVR, including sneezing, coughing, runny eyes, nasal discharge, salivation, and sometimes a slight rise in body temperature. Antibiotics and antihistamines, prescribed by your veterinarian, will help eliminate pneumonitis, although it may take a few weeks for complete recovery. Early medical treatment, as with any disease, is important. Be certain to have your Maine Coon kitten vaccinated against this infectious disease.

Feline Leukemia Virus (FeLV)—The virus FeLV causes certain types of cancer in cats, particularly cancer of the white blood cells (leukemia) and cancer of the lymph tissue cells (lymphosarcoma). Although there has been a great deal of research done on this disease, there is still no vaccine available. Some cats that are exposed to FeLV never become infected; some become infected and

Many feline viral diseases are highly contagious, especially among cats that groom each other and share the same food and water dishes and toys. Photo: Sharyn Bass.

develop immunity to the disease; others may become infected and be carriers of the disease, although they do not show signs for weeks or even years; then, of course, there are those cats who become exposed to FeLV and whose bodies cannot control the presence of the disease, so they become terminally ill.

The virus can be eliminated in the cat's saliva, urine, feces, respiratory mucus, or in the milk of a pregnant or lactating female. The disease is often spread among cats that come in close contact with each other through grooming, through sharing each other's food and water dishes, litter pans, and toys, or through scratching and biting each other. FeLV can be transmitted from a mother cat to her kittens. Although FeLV-infected queens have given birth to apparently healthy kittens, later testing often has revealed that these kittens were also infected.

143

A hearty appetite and a glowing coat generally are signs of good health. If your Maine Coon refuses to eat for more than 48 hours, consult your veterinarian. Photo: Sharyn Bass.

FeLV often lowers a cat's resistance to disease and causes a steady loss of condition, a loss of appetite, anemia, and tumors. The symptoms vary according to what organ systems have been affected. The virus can also cause other diseases, such as aplastic anemia, in which the red and white blood cells and platelets in the bone marrow are depleted.

FeLV can be diagnosed through blood tests. Usually your veterinarian will take a sample of the cat's blood and send it to a pathology laboratory where it will be determined positive or negative. If FeLV was in its early stages, the blood test may not have detected its presence, and the test will be inconclusive; it will be necessary to re-test the cat. Sometimes a cat tests negative the first time but later on tests positive. Should the test prove positive at *any* time, you must seek the advice of your veterinarian and follow his or her instructions carefully—

especially if you have more than one cat in your household. (Remember, the disease is contagious.) Incidentally, this blood test indicates only whether or not the cat is infected with the virus; it does not indicate if your cat has any of the FeLV cancers. The cancer must be detected by X-rays, palpation, or other means determined by your veterinarian.

Swift medical attention is important for those cats suspected of having FeLV. Treatment will most likely consist of any one or more of the following, depending on the severity of the disease: blood transfusions (to combat anemia), chemotherapy, vitamins, fluids, and the surgical removal of tumors. Removal of tumors, however, *does not* cure FeLV.

A healthy litter of kittens. Exercise and play are good for a cat's well being and help to tone the muscles and develop coordination and balance. Photo: Sharyn Bass.

Since there is no known vaccine available, the best thing you can do for your Maine Coon is to schedule regular check-ups with your veterinarian so that FeLV can be detected, if it is present, as early as possible. It is fervently hoped that one day a vaccine will be developed that is as effective as the other vaccines used to protect our feline friends.

Incidentally, it was once thought that there was some relationship between FeLV and human cancer. After widespread testing, there no longer is the belief or evidence that FeLV affects humans.

Feline Infectious Anemia (FIA)—This disease is caused by a microorganism that attacks and destroys healthy red blood cells. It is frequently seen in young cats between the ages of one and three (although it can affect cats of all ages) and particularly among males. Blood-sucking insects such as fleas are often carriers of the disease, so it is extremely important to keep flea infestation under control. Pregnant females also can transmit FIA within the uterus, so that the newborn kittens harbor the parasite from birth.

FIA usually occurs with other infections or when a cat's resistance to disease is low; it can also be the result of stress. Symptoms vary from mild to severe and can include any of the following: fever, loss of appetite, depression, weakness, and jaundice. In order to detect the presence of the disease, your veterinarian will have to examine a sample of your cat's blood under a microscope. Antibiotics, vitamins, and blood transfusions (in severe cases), are often prescribed.

Cats that have been neglected and have become weak, severely anemic, or jaundiced seldom survive. A well-fed, healthy, cared-for cat usually can fight off the infection. Should there be more than one cat in your household, group treatment is often necessary in order to prevent further transmission of the disease. Early detection is important; this is why a daily observation of your Maine Coon(s) is important.

Feline Infectious Peritonitis (FIP)—Feline Infectious Peritonitis is a deadly viral disease that causes an inflammation of the lining of the cat's abdomen. Both diagnosis and treatment are difficult. The disease is more common among cats than was once believed, but just how FIP is transmitted is still unknown. The "wet" form of FIP involves an accumulation of fluids in the cat's abdominal and chest cavities, and treatment by your veterinarian may include fluid extraction and the administration of antibiotics and vitamins. There are also tests available that measure the level of antibodies in the cat's blood; these tests only reveal whether the cat has been exposed to the FIP virus, and do *not* reveal if the disease is present. The "dry" form of FIP is more difficult to diagnose since the symptoms are not always obvious. There is no fluid accumulation in the dry form.

Symptoms usually develop slowly and may include fever, loss of appetite, weakness, depression, anemia, gastro-intestinal upsets, and jaundice. The abdomen becomes swollen, and there may be purulent discharges from the eyes.

Unfortunately, there is no effective cure at this time for FIP. Many cats recover from the disease and develop an immunity to the virus; however, some cats that appear to have recovered will still be carriers of the disease. Young cats, under the age of three years, are the most susceptible to FIP, although the disease can affect cats of all ages.

The disease commonly occurs in catteries and multi-cat households. The virus does not live long outside the body of an infected cat (as is the case with other viral diseases); therefore, if you lose a pet to this disease, it will be possible to bring a new cat home within a few weeks. Always check with your veterinarian first.

147

Cats, particularly males, that get into cat fights out-of-doors can be seriously injured —even castrated—by their competitors. Photo: Ron Reagan.

ABSCESSES

Cats that are allowed to roam freely out-of-doors risk getting involved in cat fights, and, as a result, are often victims of abscesses that result from scratches, bites, and puncture wounds. This is why it is important to either keep your Maine Coon indoors or in a completely closed-in area outdoors. Free-roaming males, especially, engage in combat to establish sexual superiority or to defend their territory or both, and abscesses are often seen around the tail of a young tomcat, as the older, more experienced tom tries to literally castrate his competitor.

Abscesses are pockets of infection that contain pus, and they should be treated immediately by your veterinarian so that further infection does not develop. Symptoms include swelling of the skin, fever, loss of appetite, and, of course, irritability (these pustules can be quite painful). Abscesses that are neglected can result in septicemia (blood poisoning), which can damage vital organs; abscesses found on the outer extremities such as the legs may cause bone infections, which may necessitate amputation of the infected limb; and abscesses of the ear can spread to the brain and cause a slow, painful death. These infections should not be taken lightly; in felines, abscesses are a more serious problem than one realizes.

Treatment probably will include the administration of antibiotics and surgical draining of the fluid (in severe cases). The sooner an abscess is discovered, the better the chances are of recovery for your cat.

RINGWORM

Despite its name, ringworm is a highly contagious fungal disease spread among mammals, including humans, and it is *not* caused by worms. The infection begins as tiny, bare round or oval patches, and gradually they increase in size and scabs may form. Ringworm can appear on any part of the cat's body; however, it is most often noticeable on the cat's head, neck, and legs. If you suspect your Maine Coon has contracted ringworm, call your veterinarian immediately. He or she will have to check your cat under a special ultraviolet light in order to confirm the presence of ringworm. Oral antibiotics and antifungal preparations probably will be recommended. Prompt medical attention is important to prevent the disease from spreading. Wear rubber gloves when handling your infected cat.

APPROACHING OLD AGE

Just as humans age, so will your cat. The Maine Coon Cat is a hardy breed; this, aided by the advancement of medical knowledge, will allow your cat to live to a ripe old age. A cat that has been to the veterinarian regularly for checkups and inoculations and has been properly cared for, can perhaps reach the age of 20 years.

The enjoyment of a child sharing his or her life with a pet from kindergarten through high school . . . the comfort of older people and their pets enjoying the companionship of old age together . . . for whatever reason you brought your Maine Coon into your home, the responsibility for its care moved in at the same time. Both you and your Maine Coon have formed a lasting bond of love. Your pet has repaid you doublefold the love and care you have supplied.

Now that your cat is older, it is especially important to care for its meager needs while remembering such a loyal member of your household for all those many years. As your pet ages, you must make a few changes in routine for its well-being.

Some older cats will lose their vigor somewhat and enjoy lying in the sun; others will be almost as playful as ever. The luster of the cat's coat may become a bit dull and perhaps your pet will lose a few teeth, and, thus, lose its appetite. As each cat is a unique individual, there will be differences in the pattern of aging.

No matter what befalls your pet, please give your cat all the attention and care possible as the reward for the many loving years it spent with you. At times, the cat's bladder or kidneys may deteriorate and you may have more cleaning to do because the cat's muscles cannot function as they used to. (This can also happen to humans, so have compassion for your pet's problems.)

An older cat should not be allowed to become wet or be in damp surroundings because a chill could cause illness. Many cats become plagued with rheumatism, which can be very painful in damp weather.

Should your Maine Coon have lost its teeth, its food must be minced or soft. This will help your cat retain its appetite for proper nourishment, which is important in old age. Perhaps offering baby foods, such as strained beef or chicken, may prove to be an attractive inducement, and perhaps it will become necessary for your veterinarian to occasionally clean your cat's remaining teeth.

If your older Maine Coon suffers from diarrhea, milk must be given only in very small portions as a small treat. If constipation sets in, vegetable or mineral oil should be added to the food.

Should your cat become very slow-moving, it may be wise to supply an extra litter box or two close to its favorite resting places. This will help to keep your pet from making uncontrollable mistakes.

Aging humans require more rest and so will your Maine Coon. Do not be worried if your cat should spend most of the time sleeping. It is merely an indication of the body slowing down with old age.

Regular checkups at your veterinarian's office, extra vitamins and minerals, a good diet, and extra affection can add years to your pet's life. And remember that your Maine Coon as a "senior citizen" should not be left outside unattended. Vision, hearing, and reaction time will not be the same as they were when your cat was young. Even if your cat was previously allowed outside, it will

With proper care, your Maine Coon may live to be perhaps 20 years old. Remember that as your cat approaches old age, its reflexes will slow down, its sight and hearing may diminish, and it will become less active. Photo: Sharyn Bass.

Aging cats should not be allowed outside because their ability to defend themselves will have weakened. Provide your Maine Coon "senior citizen" with a warm, comfortable place inside in which to rest. Photo: Ron Reagan.

not be able to ward off or escape dangers as well now. At this time of life, your cat will probably be more content napping quietly inside the safety of its lifelong home.

Should your beloved feline become so incapacitated that it can no longer effectively function, request the counsel of your veterinarian. Follow his or her advice, as you have done many times before, no matter how heartbreaking it may be. Your cat's welfare must be considered first, regardless of the sorrow you may feel. Do not allow your four-footed senior citizen to suffer unduly; rather, allow your pet to finally rest, free from lingering pain. If you have properly taken care of your Maine Coon and provided a safe and comfortable home for it during its lifetime, you can be certain that your pet lived a healthy and happy life.

The Future of the Maine Coon Cat

The Maine Coon Cat remains one of the hardiest of domestic felines, having for so long withstood the ravages of time and environment. There is no doubt that the breed will continue to prosper and to achieve greater popularity throughout the coming years.

But with popularity comes danger, the source of that danger being, ironically, our cat's best friend and greatest admirer—man the cat-lover. What has preserved the breed in its traditional robust form is that it has, so far, attracted a relatively small number of fanciers. Now, with its greater popularity, there are more fanciers tempted to experiment with bloodlines.

As previously discussed, every part of the Maine Coon's body serves a natural, protective function. Although not all these characteristics may be necessary in the modern world, they ought not be altered simply because breeders or judges would like to see supposed "improvements." To do so would negatively affect the hardiness and the attractiveness of the breed.

All breeds are changed once man begins to prefer certain characteristics over others—often resulting in a weakness of the strain and in an animal that could not possibly survive under the same conditions as its ancestors once did. Any animal (except perhaps livestock) that is made weaker than its ancestors cannot be considered an "accomplishment."

A breed as robust and beautiful as the Maine Coon Cat will surely continue to stir interest among cat lovers everywhere in the years to come. Photo: Ron Reagan.

For an animal as magnificent as the Maine Coon Cat to be arbitrarily tampered with for the vain satisfaction of breeders, judges, or wrongly-named "cat lovers," would be tantamount to killing it. *That must never happen!* It is this fervent hope that brings this book to a close, that the Maine Coon Cat will survive man as proudly as it survived the wilderness of times gone by.

INDEX